FOR ALL TWELVE SIGNS OF THE ZODIAC

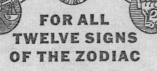

Star Guide

to self-understanding, and to understanding others. Find out about the opportunities, business prospects, and true romantic interests of those whose lives touch yours. Find out which people you are most compatible with. Achieve happiness and a harmonious life by following the stars.

AN ESSANDESS SPECIAL EDITION
New York

ISBN: 0-671-83011-2
Copyright © 1958 by Zodiac International.
All rights reserved.

Published by *Essandess Special Editions*,
a Simon & Schuster Division of
GULF & WESTERN CORPORATION
1230 Avenue of the Americas,
New York, N.Y. 10020
Trademarks registered in the United States
and other countries.

Printed in the U.S.A.

1979 Printing

PLEASE NOTE!

If you are interested in a more
detailed daily and monthly
forecast for 1980, there are
individual books for all twelve
signs of the Zodiac!

ZODIAC
CHARACTER
ANALYSIS

Dear Reader,

Modern astrology maintains that human beings have personal characteristics which are related to the position of the planets, otherwise called heavenly bodies, at the time of their birth. Planets are formed of cosmic materials. Without doubt, we also are formed of cosmic materials, chemically and physically, and therefore the cosmic forces contained in the planets exert a certain influence over us.

The cosmic mass we call Earth draws us to itself—towards its center—according to Newton's Law of Gravity. The cosmic mass we call the Sun warms us, and warmth and heat have a definite influence on the existence of life in all its forms. The Moon, too, has certain influences on us. Affliction brought on by the Moon is an officially acknowledged medical fact.

The Moon causes the ebb and flow of the tide, as every child knows. As we say, it influences water. It is well known that the human body consists of about 70 percent water; is it, therefore, not unlikely that the position of the Moon influences our bodies?

Modern science is daily gaining more information about space and time, and it will not be long until a deeper insight and correct knowledge of the conditions prevailing on other planets will be achieved, and a firm scientific basis for a new radiation theory will be found. There is every likelihood that what astrology calls "influences" will be proved correct, despite unbelieving and belittling so-called "logical minds" who do not even concede the possibility of doubt. The word IMPOSSIBLE has disappeared in the Electronic and Space Travel Age.

Necessarily, the outlines of character have to be brief. It is true that there are many surface variations among people born under each sign but, basically, they all have the same approach to life.

However, it should be noted that, as soon as a child is born, its environment begins to modify its character and, naturally, the reaction of any person will differ vitally in accordance with his education and upbringing.

We all have certain qualities which, according to our environment, develop in a positive or negative manner. Thus, selfishness may emerge as unselfishness; kindness and consideration become cruelty and a lack of consideration for others; and a naturally constructive person may, through frustration, become destructive. The latent characteristics with which we were born can, therefore, through environment and training, become something superficially different, and so apparently give the lie to the astrologer's description of the character. Yet the true character will be buried deep beneath the superficialities.

Without doubt, you have found in your life in the past—and most certainly you will find in the future—that in human relations you get on very well with certain people, whereas you just "cannot stand" others. The causes seem inexplicable to you. There is also the phenomenon of "love at first sight," which seems also to be unexplainable. People seem sympathetic or unsympathetic to each other for no obvious reason. This applies to both sexes. You might have observed that of two people who get on very well with each other, one gets on very well with a third person, whereas the other is adverse to the third person, again for no obvious reason.

People born under different Zodiacal signs are either compatible or incompatible with each other. In other words, there are good and bad interrelating factors among the different signs. You will find under your character analysis signs which are compatible with your sign.

Naturally, if all this were always accurate, humanity would be divided into groups of hostile camps. This is not so. It would be quite wrong to be hostile or indifferent to people who are born under a sign not compatible with your sign. There is no reason why you should not learn to control or adjust your feelings and actions, especially since you can become aware of the positive qualities of other people by studying their character analysis. There is no one absolutely good or absolutely bad in the true sense of the word "absolute."

Astrology, if intelligently applied, can be of the greatest help and can render you good service. It is not fortune-telling or a philosophy of predestination. It cannot be repeated often enough that the nature of man is born in him, but his own free will determines whether he will make really good use of his talents and abilities, whether he will overcome his vices or allow them to rule him.

We all know that sometimes we are born with a streak of laziness, irritability, or some other fault in our natures.

It is up to us to see that we exert enough will power to control our failings so that they do not influence us or anybody else. Through astrology our failings become apparent and we set about to rectify them. Our responsibility is in no way decreased by astrology's revelation of these traits.

Astrological interpretations bring out inclinations and tendencies, not shortcomings that are impossible to change. The horoscope of a man may show him to have criminal leanings. It does not mean that he will become a criminal.

The ordinary man finds it difficult to know himself. He is often bewildered. Astrology can frequently tell him more about himself than the different schools of psychology are able to do. Knowing his failures and shortcomings, he will do his best to overcome them and make himself a more useful member of society and a helpmate to his family. It can also save him a great deal of unhappiness and remorse.

The Prophets of the Bible refer to stars, planets and astrologers many times throughout this greatest of all books. In Ecclesiastes 3:1-8 you will find:

To everything there is a season, and a time to every purpose under the heaven:

A time to be born, and a time to die; a time to plant, and a time to pluck up that which is planted;

A time to kill, and a time to heal; a time to break down, and a time to build up;

A time to weep, and a time to laugh; a time to mourn, and a time to dance;

A time to cast away stones, and a time to gather stones together; a time to embrace, and a time to refrain from embracing;

A time to get, and a time to lose; a time to keep, and a time to cast away;

A time to rend, and a time to sew; a time to keep silence, and a time to speak;

A time to love, and a time to hate; a time of war, and a time of peace.

Aries

CHARACTER ANALYSIS FOR PEOPLE BORN BETWEEN MARCH 21—APRIL 20

ARIES ENDOWS you with a strong desire to be first and the ability for bold, dashing action. It is the sign of the go-getter. Your pioneering instinct is strong and you go plunging ahead without fear or favor. You have a great deal of ambition, and opposition spurs you on to greater effort. Your enthusiasm is great and draws people to you so that they want to follow your leadership. You are enterprising and impulsive, and your best characteristics are strength and energy. Action is your key word and you aim high. You step out with confidence and are seldom bothered by feelings of inferiority. Provided you direct your energies properly, you will go far. It takes energy to go places and you have plenty of it.

Believing that a good front is necessary, you are particular about your appearance and meticulous with your dress. No matter how few clothes you have, you always look neat and fresh because you keep your things clean and well pressed. When you step out in the morning, you look and act like a person with authority.

Your vigor and efforts are usually devoted to sensible and useful ends, and you can achieve much as a reformer and champion of the weak. You will not hesitate to change what you do not like, and you do not sit and wait for the good things of life to come to you. You will go out to grasp opportunities and enthusiastically look for them. You love to be first to start things, and any difficulties seem to give you more strength. You realize that to get things done you may have to do them yourself, for others will not always see eye to eye with you. Ambitious activities do not always yield swift results, so be content to bide your time.

Your mind is quick and full of ideas. You are on your toes and can deal with any situation or emergency. Expediency is one of your greatest assets. You can make important decisions, and nothing is ever too hard for you to tackle. Sometimes you become sidetracked because you cannot concentrate on one thing at a time. This is why you frequently make a hash of things.

Sometimes you do not use your abilities carefully and may be too easily drawn into a quarrel through your inability to see other people's points of view. You tend to underestimate others and your daring becomes useless when it is headstrong and hasty. At times, in your desire to rush things along, you overstep the mark and become overoptimistic and wildly enthusiastic for no reason at all. Your enthusiasm goes just as quickly as it comes. You rarely look before you leap and, at some time or other, do foolish things without thinking. You should mark time until your ideas have crystallized to the point where you can exploit them effectively and safely.

You have a quick temper, but it is not generally vindictive. It will flare up but will be over quickly and forgotten. Your love affairs are likely to flare up and then die out just as quickly.

Having a bold, forward nature, you are extremely independent and often proud and arrogant. You resent criticism and opposition and give way to your weaknesses to become the victim of anyone who challenges you. You can cause bad feeling by pressing issues too swiftly. Use more judgment in a clash of opinions, and try to see both sides of the question. Above all, avoid overdoing things physically, financially or otherwise.

YOUR HEALTH: You usually enjoy good health. You have a strong constitution but it is somewhat delicate. People born under your sign frequently have a healthy body, so take care of it. Aries people are especially prone to accidents, particularly to the head and face. You should exercise special care when traveling in anything fast-moving, and also in sports where there is an element of risk.

Manliness is common in Aries. And women born under this sign are often very beautiful, with long limbs and no excess flesh. Sometimes they are typical sports girls. All Aries people are good at sports and capable of sudden spurts of energy but their endurance is not great. For instance, you prefer one quick set of tennis rather than a longer match.

Your sign rules the head, and physically your nerves are your weakness, particularly of the head and stomach. You are prone to headaches, migraine and fevers. As you are impulsive and sometimes headstrong, you should beware of accidents. Breakdowns from overwork are your greatest danger. Worry, excitement and anger tend to upset your general health. You must learn to relax and control your feelings. You need rest, sleep and good food, with plenty of vegetables. You are more likely to live through diseases and fevers than others. You become impatient of sickness and recover quickly from illness. Your driving qualities make you impatient to get moving again, and there is every chance that you will lead an active life for a long time. However, as you do not do things halfheartedly, you should be careful of excessive food and drink. Although youthful qualities may remain with you until old age, you may wear yourself out before your time. You can lengthen your life if you slow your pace and tone things down as the years go by.

YOUR WORK: You have certain capabilities and talents, as we all have. The sign of Aries is connected with fire and metals so that your interests may be related to these elements: engineering, mechanical work, and various occupations which employ metal, such as armaments and war materials. You should find out what field you are most talented in and look for work there. The urge to get on in the world will lead you to jobs with good prospects. Aries rules the head and the intelligence. You are creative, ambitious and aggressive. Although you may quarrel with authority quite often, once you have accepted orders you carry them out with energy and enthusiasm. Many positions will attract, and you will have to be a little careful not to jump from one thing to another. Large concerns and growing enterprises need people with your personality and ingenuity. They will offer scope for your interest and enthusiasm and provide opportunities for your talents.

You are best suited for a job where you meet people. You are clever and quick at repartee and can make good use of it. A position with authority is ideal. You will make good wherever there is the need for someone with qualities of leadership, such as a foreman or supervisor. You are a natural leader, having the courage, energy and originality necessary to spur others to action.

Arians make good doctors, engineers and dentists. You are a man of action, excellent as a soldier and ideal for the "commander-in-the-field." You are "tough." You have courage, stamina and resourcefulness.

Collective work does not agree with you, as you are a complete individualist. You must be the leader of the team, so that you can plan to your heart's content. On the whole, you are pretty easily pleased with what you do and, as long as the concern you work for is up-to-date in its methods and outlook, you will be satisfied.

Beginning projects and schemes and leaving the finishing to others is also part of the Aries character. Arians start great things, but other great ideas inspire them before their work is completed. An Aries person with the will to stick to a task until it is finished has many opportunities in life.

MONEY: Although you are not entirely absorbed in amassing wealth, you realize the pleasure that money and the material things in life can bring. You are very active in making, spending and giving money. And you do have a good conception of how to get value for your money. You are honest in money dealings and are successful in whatever you undertake because you have the necessary drive.

Set yourself a goal and you will have the push to reach it. You like your clothes and furnishings to be fashionable, so that it is important that you have the money on hand to buy them. A generally luxurious front makes you feel powerful and confident, and more able to succeed in your work. Sometimes, you are extravagant and careless, buying when you should save and being reckless in rash investments. "Today we live, tomorrow we die," you say with bravado, and you certainly enjoy living. You should take more care in balancing your budget and watch your spending. You will probably make money slowly, and you should help it along by not acting impulsively or making quick decisions.

YOUR HOME: You are a real home-lover and family man at heart, and you like to have children around you. You look for security in a home, are handy about the house and work hard to beautify it. You show good taste here and have a keen sense of color. You want to make your home a place where you can completely relax and be happy. You cannot bear to be restrained and need complete freedom for real happiness. You are an excellent host or hostess and like your friends to drop in any time. As you are such good company, they are always pleased to come, and you are never lacking in friends who think highly of you and your home. Arians often separate from the parents' home early in life to escape the parental authority.

FRIENDSHIPS: Aries men and women are usually generous friends. You like to have many friends, especially new ones, and it is easy for you to strike up a fresh acquaintance. You are always ready to replace the old with the new, and this applies to your friendships. You make them spontaneously and they are intimate. Sometimes these kinds of friendships become too close; you become very fond of people and place them on a pedestal. Should anyone else show them attention, you become very jealous and possessive. You bully them and they are hurt. Another way you lose your friends is by treating them carelessly, or by being indiscreet with the little intimacies they pass on to you. You also have to be careful not to speak too abruptly or impatiently. On the whole, you do not take the trouble to analyze your fellow man, which is necessary if you are to know how to make lasting friendships.

ROMANCE: You are as enthusiastic and energetic in love as you are in everything else you do. You are eager for affection and need it for that extra confidence that will make you a true success in life. Those near and dear to you are very important. You are good-natured in a rough kind of way, but your charm and personality make you very attractive to the opposite sex. You are not a dreamer where love is concerned. Instead, you take practical steps to gain this essential. Your head tells you that you need lasting affection, but you also want freedom and adventure in love. To be really happy, you will have to realize that you cannot have both.

Often the Aries man is handsome but unapproachable and acts "hard-to-get." He is inclined to be very conventional in love but will allow no one to advise him. You have to guard against being too ardent, passionate or selfish. The Aries woman is extremely active in love and more unhampered in following her desires. The clean, proud appearance of such a woman is most attractive to important men. In many respects she is a good deal of a "free lance." For all of you, a little softening of the Aries nature would be a good thing, for Aries people are hard to live with. They are often so demanding and aggressive that the strain of keeping pace with them is very great.

If your romances do not turn out for the best, it may be on account of your impatience, rashness, temper and the many emotional storms which you both have to weather.

You have a flair for romance and are passionate and spontaneous. There are no halfway measures for you where love is concerned. Your whole heart and soul are in it. You like to take the lead in your love affairs right from the start. You are likely to have many of them, as you are flirtatious and fickle. You have a roving eye and a new love will charm and amuse you. If it lasts, it is because the object of your affection is so "sold" on you that he or she keeps you completely delighted. Should you launch into a fresh romance, an old love will have to take a back seat. There does not seem to be anything "foreverafter" about your love until you have found the "right" one—then your love is lasting.

MARRIAGE: It is a mistake to contemplate this in the same light as your flirtations. This must be permanent, and you must give yourself plenty of time to lay the basis for a lasting partnership. Be careful before you take the big step and do not do anything on the spur of the moment. This is one occasion where you cannot afford to make a rash decision or much harm will be done to you and to the other person involved. Many Arians do not know themselves until full maturity, when it is undoubtedly safest to contemplate matrimony.

More than one marriage is often necessary to find happiness for the Aries man or woman. They are not easy to live with and when young often make unsuitable selections of sweethearts or mates. If events make it possible for them to make a choice when they are about thirty-five years old, the chances of choosing wisely are good. The vitality to marriage which they contribute makes them interesting partners.

As you are a positive type, the best partner for you is a quiet and adoring one who is a foil for your aggressive ways. There is less chance of finding happiness if you are married to a type similar to yourself. It would probably mean only continual bickering, with marriage becoming one argument after another. This clash of characters leads to emotional interplay and, naturally, to a certain amount of tension and strain. You could easily carry this too far. However, the satisfaction and enjoyment of making up could become a binding factor.

Your partner will draw upon your energy and find you a source of vitality and inspiration. You, in turn, will gain something from him or her and grow mentally and emotionally. The right mate can make you and your marriage a success. Changing your partner to suit yourself will be your natural inclination, but it is better to adjust yourself. It is a case of give and take on both sides. Be sure to give as well as take, and happiness is yours.

THE ARIES HUSBAND is a very desirable partner, for he is ardent, proud and full of personality, which continues his romantic appeal all through life. But, by appearance and temperament, he is a little hard to acquire. He is a bit fussy and precise about what he wants. He has a romantic, idealized picture of what he wants in a wife, and all too often expects perfection. She must be beautiful, clever and very good. He has a rather conventional outlook regarding marriage and does not tolerate anything but strictly correct behavior. He expects to be treated as the head of the household and wants his wife and home to reflect his success and ability.

THE ARIES WIFE is a good mother and fine housekeeper and a wonderful partner for an ambitous man. She is witty, a clever conversationalist and socially-minded. She generally has a fine, independent mind, and, if she is not willing to help her husband in business, may have some sideline of her own. This may be a rather unusual outlet for she is an unconventional woman. She is efficient, wide-awake, generous and companionable.

Pride is one of her outstanding qualities; pride not only in her appearance but in her home and family. Sometimes she may cause jealousy and resentment by making it plain to others that she considers her own family far superior.

Her worst faults are jealousy and a desire for a competitive social life. She knows that she is good and wants her husband to give all his attention to her and never praise anyone else. She shines at all social functions and is particularly capable as the guiding hand in any important gathering, putting people at ease and making introductions. In society the Aries woman is at her best. She is completely at ease, witty and has terrific vitality.

She is well suited to a very possessive man and is capable of great self-sacrifice for her family. If she marries a retiring man, she would be too overpowering and submerge him in her activities in the home and with her boundless affection. An aggressively masculine man suits her best; she loves only the man she can greatly admire and would be a great asset to him. His ability to control her is an important part of her devotion to him and he must be sure to keep her esteem. She is his for life if he lets her look up to him and keeps a dominant hold of the household.

CHILDREN: Although you would rather not be tied down by responsibilities, to be childless is unnatural for you. You are delighted to have children and your children are delighted with you and your bright, youthful personality. You are at ease with them and understand their ways. They find your youthful good spirits great fun and your liking for practical jokes delights them. Your affectionate teasing also adds to their fun. (Boys born in Aries are often the leaders of the pranks at school or camp, and will be rough rather than cruel.) Older children accept you as one of the gang and you are always ready to play with them. They will let you beat them at a game if it means you will play with them again.

However, you must exercise restraint in planning your children's careers, as you may dictate to them. You are inclined to become overbearing if the family does not measure up to your standards or will not accept your opinion as the final word. Social prominence is all-important and you are happiest when your children are in the spotlight.

By now you are well aware that there are good and bad aspects to everyone's character, and that we can react to them or rectify them to our benefit.

If you are a good type of Arian, you may have the following characteristics:

POSITIVE QUALITIES: Strength and energy are your greatest assets, combined with generosity. You have plenty of personality and inspiration and you use your head. Brain, not muscle, is your driving power. A person of enterprise and plenty of go, you are a born leader and inspire others to action. Your enthusiasm and zest for living are catching and others will follow you. You meet life's challenges with vigor and even seem to thrive on them. Your policy is to attack life, to keep moving—not to wait for it to come to you. You have little time for the negative, slow approach to life. For you, it is busy and interesting and you like it to be fast and furious. In spite of this urge to do everything quickly, you do not wear out, because you thrive on it and generate new life and energy.

You could not care less about old age or that "rainy day" for they never catch up with you. Your youthful qualities keep you young and hopeful. Although you are sometimes down, it is not for long. You have the courage to overcome all setbacks and you soon regain your sense of humor.

On the other hand, the lesser type of Arian may have these characteristics:

NEGATIVE QUALITIES: Like others, you have your faults. In your brisk way you may say what you think and are not always discreet and tactful. You are impatient and too quick to be thorough. For you it is more important to do things quickly and forcefully than to be careful how you do them or how they will turn out.

You may find it very difficult to be impartial. You have to go all the way; there is nothing halfhearted about you. If things do not come your way, you will become restless and moody and go "looking for a fight." Then you are temperamental, pigheaded, rude and inconsiderate. You can be very sarcastic and abrupt in what you say and do. You have a sudden change of humor and are a totally different person.

It is important for you to keep your strong egotistical qualities to the fore. A reversal of form or change of events may find you nervous, timid and halting, afraid or "yellow." Conflicting forces within yourself as the result of some emotional experience or destructive influence may bring this side of your personality to light, with disastrous results. Instinctively you know that things are not right and that you are not your real self. You must rid yourself of the emotional block or whatever it is that is holding you back. The remedy is up to you.

Aries compatible with Taurus, Gemini, Leo, Sagittarius, Aquarius and Pisces.

Incompatible with Cancer, Libra and Capricorn.

Taurus

CHARACTER ANALYSIS
FOR PEOPLE BORN BETWEEN
APRIL 21 — MAY 20

YOU ARE the strong, silent type of person who always has both feet on the ground and knows where he is going. Of all the types you are the most patient and will work and wait for anything you happen to want, especially money or love. A stubborn streak is noticeable in your nature and you can become very determined. Your tenacity is your strongest potential; insults and destructive criticism have not the slightest effect on you. You push aside obstacles and wear down opposition with your steady and relentless striving.

You are exactly opposite to people who are high-strung. You often appear to have no nerves. You are slow, steady, practical and reserved. You keep your plans to yourself and resist change. Your temper is peaceful and not easily aroused, but once provoked, you can be violent and unrelenting. As a rule you are long-suffering and put up with a lot, but it is dangerous for others to deliberately make you angry. Sometimes a small irritation will be a fuse which ignites your anger into fury.

Your nature is somewhat stolid: outwardly placid and conservative. You are a plodder to the utmost degree. Anything you do is deliberate and based on decisions well thought out beforehand. You will bide your time until you feel it is wise to act. Then you allow nothing to stand in your way.

You like comfort and ease and will work hard to obtain them. Material possessions give you confidence, for you are generally timid and may suffer from an inferiority complex. Once you realize that you have great strength of character, you will lose this. You are inclined to feel that others are constantly measuring you by what you have. And, being proud, you have to build up your reputation by building up your material goods.

You are loyal and trustworthy and, on the whole, easy to get along with. You admire success and are ready to support it, but dislike misery and instinctively draw away from it. You are ambitious, and once you set your heart on something, you can be very industrious and capable of concentrated effort.

Your whole nature is uncomplicated, and everything you do and say is straightforward and natural. You are slightly skeptical of anything that is sophisticated and you like to see things clearly and have all the details at your fingertips. You have a very down-to-earth mind and, once it is made up, it is very difficult to change it. You seldom jump to conclusions or take people or conditions at their face value. When you finally reach an opinion, one can depend upon it to be unbiased and honest.

YOUR HEALTH: In appearance, you are inclined to be stocky, broad-shouldered, and have a good deal of physical strength. Women born under this sign usually have a good deal of physical beauty and graciousness with a charming delicacy. Both men and women have clear complexions. You blush easily and your eyes usually sparkle with good health.

Your health is naturally robust and you seem, at times, to have superhuman strength and energy. Often you are less sensitive to pain than many people and can stand up to stress and strain better than others. You do not like to admit to a physical disability and are not at all happy when illness comes your way. You regard it as a weakness and, would rather suffer as long as you can before having to admit it. Your endurance is great and it takes a lot to get you down. Your recovery is likely to take longer than another's because your recuperative power does not act quickly, but it is strong even if slow.

Your throat is the part of the body most susceptible to weakness, and it plays an important part in your make-up. You have a fine singing voice; some of the world's best singers have been Taureans. You seem to get more colds than anyone else and should not neglect any symptoms, especially pertaining to your throat. You will be wise to avoid fats and food which heats up the blood. You will also have to be more moderate than others with food and drink. Often quantity is more important than quality and you put on excess weight more easily than people of other signs.

YOUR WORK: You can cope with most jobs, given the proper training. You are always methodical and may be slow at first; in your school days you do not pick things up quickly, but what you learn you do not readily forget. As a rule, you are not outstandingly intelligent, but when it comes to shrewdness and tenacity in business you shine.

Your incentive makes you look to firm and reliable foundations in business and you like safe and well-tried methods in all your dealings. You do not take chances and like to foresee every step of the way. In doing this, you run the danger of getting into a rut if you are not careful. Like a good builder, you make sure that your foundation is strong before constructing the superstructure. You want things to last and endure a long time.

You make a good administrator and can easily keep order and discipline. You are able to control others through your own self-control and inflexibility of purpose. You do not yield readily to opposition in your work, and once you have made a decision, you are hard to budge.

You give great attention to detail in your work, and are patient, conservative and constructive. Suitable jobs for you are those requiring painstaking, unhurried effort. Routine managership, architecture, and industrial, technical and statistical work would suit you.

Creative work is always part of the Taurean temperament, because you have an eye for beauty and what is likely to please the senses. But often you have difficulty giving it expression due to circumstances and environment. Given the opportunity, you may even make a lifework of some branch of the arts to which you have always been inclined.

Your urge to live in the country is very strong and, if you find your occupation there, well and good. You would make an excellent large-scale farmer, and might successfully go in for fruit growing or livestock and poultry raising. You are a great experimenter, particularly in growing things.

Sometimes you may hold a subordinate position, but this does not lower your morale. You enjoy serving and are faithful to the end. You have the ability to earn money for others and are good at executive work. You are content to work for others if you enjoy what you are doing and you will carry out instructions carefully and in complete detail.

Should you have a partner in your work, it would not be wise for him to suddenly confront you with a new idea. He should, rather, carefully plant the seed in your mind, allowing you to accept the idea gradually. You usually come to regard it as your own and put it into practice.

MONEY: Taurus is the money sign of the Zodiac. You are likely to worship money and the things it will buy. It is fortunate that you have the gifts of patience and endurance to pursue wealth until you get it. But if this goal gets too firm a hold on you, you may become greedy. You may develop a very materialistic outlook and place too high a value on money.

The ideals which drive you are somewhat linked with the factor of possessions and the desire to build up an estate. Even if you are an ordinary business man striving to accumulate money, or a banker with ideas mainly concerned with money, a backlog will be an incentive.

You are generally upright and practical in regard to money and will never refuse requests for financial help. In your youth, you can be cautious with money and should beware of hoarding it. But once you have made your fortune, you spend more freely. You do not usually live up to every penny of your income, but always like to keep a portion in reserve. Therefore, you are seldom completely broke. You do not take financial risks, or squander your money unnecessarily, and there are times when you can be extremely lucky. You are temperamently suited to gambling and you often win, for you have steady nerves, great perseverance and can easily put on a "poker face."

Material status is the end for which you work, and it is the standard by which you measure your success. The best paid jobs attract you, particularly in the luxury trades, for you like all that makes life easy and like to enjoy it to the full.

FRIENDSHIPS: You are usually loyal to your friends; you are warmhearted and faithful. People will seek you out as a friend, for they like to bask in the warmth of your friendship and companionship, and they admire the sincerity of your sympathy.

You are always ready to give advice, which is usually based upon conservative thinking. It is unfortunate that sometimes you choose wealthy and prominent friends in preference to those who may be poor and obscure. You always like to be associated with affluent and popular people. Influential friends are likely to prove helpful, but you should take care that those who mean well do not break up your domestic happiness.

You appear so gentle and kindly that it may seem impossible to anger you, and sometimes people presume too far and find themselves engulfed in your seemingly irrational fury. Your enemies can be as detrimental as your friends can be thoughtful. You may make some enemies through your uncompromising and dogmatic nature.

ROMANCE: You have a natural outlook on love and can easily attract love affairs. Although you may have many romances, once you fall in love it is for good. You are naturally inclined to faithfulness in love and your emotions are deep. Your nature is basically passionate but you are very direct in your approach. You are quiet but underneath this you can be jealous and possessive. You need more idealism and less of the practical approach to marriage.

You are more calculating than impulsive, and once you have made up your mind that a certain person is your ideal, you will leave no stone unturned until you gain the object of your choice. You look for inner qualities in the one you love and take your time in making your decision. You need steadfast love and warm affection and are capable of returning these qualities.

MARRIAGE: You look forward to marriage and security, for it means you have someone to possess and belong to. Marriage means permanency to you, and Taureans make loving wives and devoted husbands. Love is very real to you and, although you are conscious of the physical charms of the opposite sex, you take your legal responsibilities very seriously. You will always fulfill your social and financial obligations.

Both sexes are naturally suited for matrimony and domestic life. Although your thoughts sometimes stray to other things, you never forget what is required of you in a material way. You are affectionate, warm and loving, and, although you may look for variety in affection at times, its absence does not upset you. You are easy to get along with as long as you are treated fairly. You can be bluntly sarcastic to your partner but hate confusion and quarreling.

THE TAURUS HUSBAND has all the qualities necessary for success in marriage. He adores his wife and children, and makes every effort to give them all the necessities and comforts that he can. He wants his family to have the best home and his children to have a fine education. He may marry into a class above him because he is ambitious to establish himself. If he is successful, he will want to go on to higher social circles.

Sometimes the violence of his emotional nature comes to the fore, but it is counteracted by his reliability, generosity and faithfulness. Any outside interest that he may allow to intrude into his domestic routine is often only a fleeting one, and he never really neglects his home. But he does like to be the boss and may resent his wife's attempts to direct his affairs.

He has a keen appreciation of beauty and, in order to hold his attention through life, his wife must always look attractive. He loves to be depended upon and likes to feel that he is the sole provider and is responsible for his family's happiness. He seldom finds domestic life tiresome and never regrets his marriage. Unlike most men, he does not think back regretfully to the days when he was free to do as he pleased.

THE TAURUS WIFE has a pleasant disposition, responds to kind treatment and is flattered by luxury. Her strong qualities are contentment, consideration and service, which are revealed when she marries a well-to-do man. She is not so much mercenary, but has, rather, a thorough knowledge of herself. She may be beautiful and possess outstanding qualities, and she has learned to place a value on herself. It is not so much vanity, either, but rather a feeling that she must be sheltered, cared for and protected. In return, the Taurus wife and mother is willing to blend into the domestic background.

She is, perhaps, the most devoted and dependable kind of wife, with a deep and abiding affection for her family. And she may surpass herself in this direction if she is satisfied with her husband's efforts on her behalf. She is "pushy" in a quiet way and likes her husband to be ambitious. Outwardly she is reserved, calm and everybody's friend, but underneath she may be jealous and very fond of the worldly things of life.

She infrequently doubts her husband's affection, largely because it seldom strays. Although she makes no secret of her love, she expects something in return. She rarely divorces and will suffer extreme hardship rather than leave her mate. Her nature is particularly adapted to domestic life, and she can be described as the ideal woman to help set up a home. But beneath all her goodness there is a persistent streak. She is determined to enjoy life, and although she can well look after herself, she goes out of her way to be very dependent.

YOUR HOME: Your home and family, and the money to support them simply and harmoniously, are very important to you. You like to be at home more than other people and are not so prone to seek recreation away from your home. Taurus men are good providers and Taurus women are good homemakers.

Your home is a happy place to live in and is usually comfortable and restful. You are a home person and like the simple things of life. You want beauty in your home, but first and foremost you must have comfort. You usually have excellent taste, especially in interior decoration. You have a fine sense of color and are a good judge of art; often you are an artist yourself.

You like the country and are fond of beautiful scenery. Your domestic routine is efficient and you have the gift of making people feel at home. Property, position and popularity mean much to you and you like to fill your home with many people. No one ever dines better than in the house of a Taurean, and you are very put out if you get fed badly when you are someone else's guest.

CHILDREN: You are strict with your children and may even appear tyrannical to them. You do not consider that your children have the same rights as you, and are careful to see that they always treat you with respect. However, you have good intentions and your children will profit by them in the long run.

You are a capable and conscientious parent who likes to lead a dignified life. Your children will bring you great pleasure and satisfaction, especially when you have brought them up properly. You have affection for them and want the best for them but you are not likely to be overindulgent.

Taurus children are stalwart, but emotional security is their greatest need. They need consistent love and encouragement. Because of their self-control, they appear self-reliant but they really suffer from overmodesty and are in danger of acquiring an inferiority complex. They should be praised more than blamed. With careful attention and much reassurance, their personalities will develop slowly but surely.

But now you are well aware that there are good and bad aspects to everyone's character, and that we can react to them or rectify them to our benefit.

If you are a strong Taureau, you may have the following characteristics:

POSITIVE QUALITIES: Although you may not be intellectual, your quiet, steadfast and conservative qualities are the greatest asset to humanity. Your conservative outlook and determination make you the sort to pick up the mistakes of others and repair the damage. You are the best of all types to see that the good ideas of others are carried out.

Your sense of color is acute and your artistic work reflects your love for harmony. Your ambition will spur you on to great heights. In material things, you soon discover the difference between good and bad and where to find the very best. You are persevering and firm, but sometimes these can be dormant virtues and you need outside stimuli to accomplish what you want.

Your life should be a successful one, without too much to disturb its harmony, unless your inborn stubbornness makes you meet obstacles head on rather then avoiding them.

On the other hand, the lesser types of Taureans may have these characteristics:

NEGATIVE QUALITIES: You can be brutishly stubborn and blind to reasoning. You dislike being contradicted and no one can ever hurry you. You may be pigheaded to the point of being overconservative and anti-progressive.

Although you are pretty definite about what you want and enthusiastic in doing it, you do nothing without reflection. You may be altogether too prudent and obstinate when your mind is made up. You are slow in making it up, but once it is made up, nothing can change it.

Your greatest weakness in life is materialism. Possessiveness can spoil much in your make-up, which is basically good. Although you are broad-minded in big things, you can be extremely narrow-minded and avaricious in small ones.

You do not trust people too easily and you can be quite suspicious of the faithfulness of others. Although you are difficult to arouse, once aroused you are even more difficult to soothe. Although you will forgive a wrong, you do not forget it easily.

You may give in to inertia and laziness. But these vices must get a real grip on you before you show obvious signs of them.

The weaker Taurus woman is often slovenly, overindulgent and "frowsy." Fortunately, the negative type is rare and it is more often the dependable, positive type that we meet in everyday life.

Taurus compatible with Gemini, Cancer, Pisces, Virgo, Capricorn and Aries.
Incompatible with Leo, Scorpio and Aquarius.

Gemini

CHARACTER ANALYSIS FOR PEOPLE BORN BETWEEN MAY 21—JUNE 20

GEMINI IS an intellectual sign, and you are motivated by your mind and thought rather than your senses. It is the sign of duality so that, more than other persons, you have two distinct natures. Your disposition is likely to change very quickly as it is like quicksilver, up and down according to the people and conditions you meet. It ranges from grave to gay, and your interests cover both the concrete and the abstract, the conscious and the subconscious, the subjective and the objective. You are sanguine by nature, fly into a temper easily, and just as easily forget all about it, not only what the other person has said but what you have said.

You are ambitious and sensitive. You have an active mind, quick perception and no trouble remembering things. Being inquisitive and wanting to know, you are always on the lookout for fresh ideas and information. You are alert and quick on the uptake, versatile and adaptable, and are likely to take on two things at the same time. You sometimes tend to spread your energies over too wide a field instead of finishing off one thing at a time. Having "too many irons in the fire" makes it difficult for you to concentrate, so that many of the projects and enterprises you take on go unfinished. Once you get over this, you are able to make the most of your fine intellectual powers. Your range of thought is very wide, although you lack mental concentration. You may achieve this as you get older, but it does not come naturally. You may store up in your mind a great many facts and bits of information which you may never put to any good use.

But if you study and learn to apply yourself, you have the intellectual power to gain enormously.

You have a talent for languages. You love books and learning, and your thirst for knowledge leads you to read a great deal. You learn easily and may be able to talk about many things, but often what you read does not sink in. Sometimes things appear very clear to you when you may, in fact, be wrong. You may prefer to sidestep the truth and enjoy a good joke instead. As you rule, you are not willing to believe what you have not seen but, once you have seen it, you can tell everybody else about it and enjoy doing so. You are open-minded about most things and it is likely that your viewpoint will be reasonable. You are always ready to understand the other man's outlook.

Gemini is pre-eminently the sign of the concrete mind that deals with facts and figures rather than with ideas and experiments. You rarely do anything without a purpose, and your ambition is restless rather than fanatical. You need to develop consistent effort and continuity of action.

YOUR HEALTH: Your body is as active as your mind, and you live, to a great extent, on your nervous energy. A sure way of ruining your health is by worrying and exhausting that nervous energy. Your weak points physically are your nerves and lungs, and you may suffer from colds, influenza or pleurisy. Your health is generally good, but you may give the appearance of being delicate, which is usually not so. If people get this impression, it may be because of your nervousness and thin physique. You seldom contract illness and it does not seem to take a strong hold on you, although the reverse may be the case when you are under strain. You are restless and your nerves will suffer if you are energetic in too many directions, so it is wise not to overtax your nerves. Your mind is always alert and you may find it difficult to sleep, but it is important that you get adequate rest. Relaxation and plenty of sleep should be part of your daily routine.

Gemini people are often good-looking, with small, neat features. They have an animated expression which indicates intelligence. They are usually slender, with a nervous and impatient manner. Their moods are likely to change very quickly, and they may become bored doing one thing and want to try something else.

YOUR WORK: You are active and industrious and like interesting and varied work. You are best suited to a job which makes full use of your intellectual leanings. You are naturally inquisitive and like talking and imparting knowledge. You have a sense of humor and an easy manner. You are a fine speaker and would be happy in any work which brings you in contact with the public. People born under this sign make good agents, brokers, merchants, secretaries and lawyers.

You are always on the alert for the better half of a bargain and make an excellent salesman. You can play with facts cleverly, and your gift of criticism would make you an efficient journalist and critic, especially a music critic. You have a talent for writing of any sort, as long as it provides you a means of expressing your own thoughts in your own way.

You are also suited for trades where great delicacy and dexterity are essential. You make fine surgeons, dentists and engineers, and are adapted to being radio mechanics or being in aeronautics, for your sign is air-minded. You are also mathematically inclined and make a good accountant. However, you have to exert yourself to continue with the studies required for these occupations.

You are loyal to your employer but prefer to work in your own way without advice or criticism. You love travel and movement, and are fond of changing employment as well as scene. But when you travel, it is not so much to enjoy the beauties and culture of other countries, but simply for the sake of moving.

You hate to concentrate on one job only and rarely stay in the first position you take. You often change three, four or five times, but when you eventually decide on something, you will stick to it and try to make it as many-sided as possible.

If you find your work dull or routine, you will feel dispirited and unhappy. You have to get fun out of your work. As you are constantly gathering knowledge and information, you are capable of doing most things, which earns you the name of "jack of all trades." You like everything modern and believe in speed.

You usually choose some well-paid business, for you are not the long-suffering type who works for nothing. You may be called mercenary, as you rate yourself very highly and demand just compensation for your efforts.

MONEY: Your changes of interest keep you buying and spending but, on the whole, security is the keynote to most of your monetary transactions. You accomplish a great deal once you discipline yourself to a planned program of economy and saving. You are always on the lookout for new ways of increasing your income, whether it be a new sideline, a better paying job, a new contract or higher pay for overtime. Sometimes you may be exposed to financial temptation, so it is better for the weaker Gemini to steer clear of jobs as cashiers and treasurers. You should also stay out of schemes or plots for making money quickly, as there is a chance of being tempted and becoming involved in money troubles of an unfortunate sort.

You often benefit from the support of influential contacts, and money is most likely to come to you through the help or advice of such contacts. Your tastes are generally modest, but they can vary to the expensive, according to your friends and feelings.

You are not stingy and cheerfully meet costs. While it is important to be emotionally and mentally receptive to change, often it is better for you to be relatively conservative. Sometimes you get carried away by a current interest and your bank account may suffer. Money may not pour in for you, but your earnings and income are generally regular and dependable.

YOUR HOME: Environment is important to you and, for a peaceful state of mind, you should be surrounded by harmony and beauty. Although home life does not appeal very strongly to you, you do not dislike it as long as it continues to be interesting.

Entertaining in your home is your great delight. Relatives, friends and business connections gravitate toward your home, which is likely to be a busy place. You can sometimes be uneconomical but, on the whole, you manage your home well. You are fond of change and make it a point to be up-to-date in all your home appliances. You like decorating. Your home is likely to be modern in style.

If you feel that your responsibilities weigh you down, you may pack your suitcase and take off. You are ever ready to move and do not like to settle down. Your adaptability makes it possible for you to be at home wherever you hang your hat. If your family burdens become frustrating, you may become morose and your home and family suffer. You like to be near people with plenty of go, so that you are kept interested and contented. If you can control your impulses, you will be more satisfied once you have made a permanent home.

You are inclined to be more concerned by what your home gives you rather than what you give your home. You are naturally a thinker, and there are many ways you can improve your home and make your family more comfortable. You try to be fair, but often you neglect your home and family in order to gratify your own desires.

FRIENDSHIPS: It is difficult to picture a Geminian alone, and this is not likely to happen. You need people with plenty of activity and movement about you. Being easy to get along with, you make many friends and few enemies. You are good company and people like to be with you. You expect others to be fair and honest in friendship and you are not likely to ever forget or forgive a wrong.

Having many sides to your nature, you need intellectual satisfaction. You can do this through meeting many types of people and by making friends in all levels of society. You do not like to sit still, but would rather be in half a dozen places at the same time, meeting people and exchanging ideas. Once you realize this is impossible, you will appreciate your present acquaintances and relax and enjoy them.

Your friends find you very lively and rather difficult to pin down. If their opinions do not suit you, you will exchange ideas with them without too much discrimination. You admire and like people who use their brains, and enjoy intellectual circles where you find people with similar interests.

Socially you are a success and have a gay and charming temperament. You add to the success of any function, for you are always witty and poised. Although you are socially popular, you cannot resist gossip. Sometimes you let your sharp tongue get the better of you. You are always on the lookout for something to discuss or criticize, for good or bad. Your friendships may suffer as a result of this.

ROMANCE: You long for love but often fail to find it for, although you make friends quickly, you just as quickly find fault with them. You are likely to be shallow in love. As you like variety in life, so you do in romance. You do not want to be tied down or feel possessed. Many love affairs give you plenty of opportunity for self-expression, which you find exciting. To give yourself entirely to one emotional experience is not your nature, and you are not inclined to devote yourself readily to one attachment. Others may find you difficult to understand, for you feel that variety is the spice of life and the more romances the better. Your changeability baffles your associates, for you feel no compunction whatever in terminating an association when it no longer interests you.

You like flirtation and are happy when there is someone near you who is responsive to your mood. You may go out of your way to make sure this is nearly always the case. Yet you are gentle and sympathetic in love, which is natural for you and not necessarily the result of careful scheming.

In Gemini men, we find the contrast of mild affection and passionate romance. As a lover you can be teasing and flirtatious but you seldom are vitally interested. Even when you are attracted, another interesting personality can quickly charm you. Your affection is ruled more by your mind than by your emotions and you seem to lack any depth of feeling. You may look upon love from the intellectual angle or may be cynical and calculating.

As a Gemini woman, you are much like the Gemini man in matters of romance, so that you appear extremely fickle and may be a sore trial to your admirers. You are always ready to listen to the other point of view, if the other person can manage to get a word in. Gemini is also the sign of the talker.

But you Gemini people should not feel that you are

entirely incapable of constancy, for you are loyal and sincere, and can fall deeply in love with the right one. You realize that there is a give-and-take involved and are quite willing to share responsibilities.

MARRIAGE: Marriage is an adventure for you which is full of interest and excitement. If you find it too binding, you may make a quick change and move out of it, but you can adapt yourself to it with great success. For marriage, your partner should have stability and adjustability. If he or she can match your wits and is on the same intellectual level, marriage will be delightful for you both.

To mates who expect real affection and emotional response, you may be a disappointment for it is difficult for you to give yourself. There may be small irritations in marriage but, as you make an amiable partner, there is not much danger of any reasons to cause serious disagreements. You will probably both find great pleasure in travel and entertainment. If he or she appreciates your alert and intuitive mind, you will both benefit from the association.

THE GEMINI HUSBAND needs a wife who can share his mental interests, is never tied to her home and is willing to change her environment as often as her husband wishes for new scenery. His wife must get used to his general interest in other people, or other women. She should not take his flirtations too seriously.

He is very often down-to-earth and can be pretty definite in bringing any romance to an end if he feels he will lose by it. He will be successful in life if his wife gives him direction without nagging. Home ties mean a lot to him, but he is temperamentally unfit to put up with constant pressure. He is quite likely to leave home if he has an overbearing wife.

THE GEMINI WIFE is first and foremost an intellectual woman; her strongest appeals are mental companionship and the ability to be a partner in living rather than a mere housekeeper. It is natural for her to keep up her outside interests after marriage, particularly if she is accomplished. Often this takes up a lot of time, which a husband may resent. If there is to be harmony, she must be more tactful. If she realizes it is impossible to lead two lives, she will gradually learn to give up one in favor of her home life.

She also has a flirtatious nature, which may worry her husband and cause him to watch her anxiously. He would be much happier if he could realize that she is using her sharp wits in a battle of words. However, her protective instinct and common sense are very strong and she would never let an affair come between her and her home and family.

Usually she is so capable that her home and outside interests are managed very smoothly. She is very particular about how her home is run, even if she is not in it as much as other wives. She is generally a refined person who dislikes untidiness. She seldom does her own work but directs efficiently and likes obedience.

CHILDREN: Others may not think you are very maternal or paternal in your attitude, and sometimes you feel children are a nuisance. You may grouch at the responsibilities they give you, but when you carry on in this fashion, your bark is invariably worse than your bite. Nevertheless, you cannot help liking children because they love you. You cannot hide the fact that you are well able to deal with them. If they come into your life, you will adapt yourself to them and try to make life as enjoyable as possible for them. You are the sort who will climb trees with them and energetically enter into their games. You are good fun and they cannot help but enjoy your company.

Gemini children are high-strung and prefer not to have the attention the ordinary child needs. Their surroundings should be as calm and peaceful as possible and nothing should be done to excite them. They require careful handling by understanding parents. They need plenty of interests to occupy their minds, which seem to be working day and night. But they should be taught to stay with one thing until it is finished. Their minds are very plastic and can be molded in the right direction by their parents. They have an unusual intuition which makes them uneasy when you are untruthful or try to force something upon them they do not think is right. You will probably be kept eternally busy answering questions and will have to exert yourself to keep one jump ahead of your Gemini child at all times.

By now you are well aware that there are good and bad aspects to everyone's character, and that we can react to them or rectify them to our benefit.

If you are a strong Geminian, you may have the following characteristics:

POSITIVE QUALITIES: Your main strength is the reasonable and logical way you set about things, which enables you to cope with any situation. You know this and have faith in yourself, even though you sense that this quality is often unappreciated.

You have an intellectual and analytical mind, but it may be impersonal, guided in its decisions, not by your emotions, but by your common sense. This is a great asset when there is need for an unbiased opinion. Because you are able to see both sides of a problem, your reasoning and quick decisions are usually logical and accurate. You are generally an optimist and rarely let things get you down.

Because you can grasp things quickly, you hate hazy or sentimental thinking which may lead to loose and incorrect conclusions. You like literature and art and anything abstract does not deter you, for you can examine it unemotionally. You have charm, grace and talent, and are able to express yourself clearly in words and action. You admire brains and cleverness, and people are impressed by your own mental vigor and agility.

On the other hand, the lesser type of Gemini may have these characteristics: -

NEGATIVE QUALITIES: Although you are usually well-informed and apparently have plenty of information on any subject mentioned, this is sometimes deceptive, for you think so quickly and speak so fluently that a superficial knowledge carries you a long way. Sometimes your lack of concentration gives you only a shallow understanding. You have the detachment and coolness of the stronger Gemini type but you may be more prone to calculated cunning. As a weaker Gemini woman, you may be a "gold digger." To everybody else, you may seem fragile and need a strong arm to lean on, whereas you may often be cold and hard underneath.

You may place too much importance on facts rather than emotions, which may make you seem heartless and cynical. Sometimes you waver a good deal and have difficulty making up your mind. Your fondness for detail often causes you to get lost in it. People may think you arrogant because you understand things better than they do; people find you without feeling. When you do show feeling, you do not do it freely and easily, and often are hard, egotistical, and selfish.

Often you are too fond of examining your own thoughts, with the result that you become self-centered, discontented and flippant with other people's feelings. If you are under severe strain, you may be untruthful, dishonest and deceitful.

It is ironical that sometimes you are so busy thinking that you do not have time to stop and think. If you occasionally put your feelings before your intellect, you would be more human. Trying to do many things at once may make you flighty when it comes to important issues. Whatever decision you make then is likely to be drastic, and any change of opinion or principle will be on the spur of the moment according to your interests. Do not be too influenced by gossip and intrigue, but stick to facts. You naturally like to know the setup and get to the bottom of things, so let this be your guiding principle.

Gemini compatible with Cancer, Leo, Libra, Aquarius, Aries, Taurus.

Incompatible with Virgo, Sagittarius, Pisces.

Cancer

CHARACTER ANALYSIS FOR PEOPLE BORN BETWEEN JUNE 21—JULY 20

OF ALL people you are the most moody, sensitive and impressionable, liking a great deal of sensation and emotion. You react more through your feelings and senses than through your mind. As a rule, you are very responsive, full of sympathy for suffering or misfortune and extremely generous. At the same time, you are often taken advantage of because you find it difficult to refuse help and are too easily influenced. You should learn to say "No" to people sometimes.

If your temper is aroused, you do not stay angry for long or harbor a grudge but if you are hurt, you can be very sharp. To offset your timidity and fear of appearing weak, you often adopt a second nature as a protection. Then you may prove rough, energetic and dictatorial, bluffing others into submission. You have great tenacity of purpose, and once your mind becomes set, you stick to an idea or position with great persistence. You are inclined to be stubborn.

You are often moody and frequently morbid, and you are prone to sensationalism. There is a danger of moral weakness because of this highly active instinct for the sensational. You may dramatize the small things which upset you emotionally, for you are susceptible to all kinds of outside influences.

You are encouraged by kindness and appreciate a pat on the back. Criticism may cause you to climb into your shell and could contribute to an inferiority complex. Because you are easily influenced, you pay far too much attention to what people might say. You worry about what you think may be said behind your back.

Your love for home is one of your chief characteristics. You enjoy all kinds of changes and are able to adapt yourself to them easily. You are naturally conventional and conservative in the best sense, although you are still interested in all that is new. This is one of the many contrasts in your nature. Your memory is always ready to take you back into the past, in which you live, while you are frequently inclined to regard the future with anxiety and misgiving. Many of your actions or ideas may be founded on the history of the past, as you are more inclined to look backward than forward.

You are invariably kind and gentle and cause one to

feel the urge to confide in you, especially those who are seeking sympathy. You will forgive almost anything, but it is not a good idea for others to hurt your feelings. Although you are vain to the extent that you attach much importance to your appearance, your vanity is more of the mind. You do not like others to think you stupid, but if they do, it is important to you that they do not show it. They should spare your feelings, for you have unusual intuition and sense what is behind their words.

You are fond of music and are fundamentally deeply religious. Your love for the secret and mysterious in life and nature is very great. Inwardly you are afraid of it and fear that it might influence you too strongly. However, you have an extremely strong urge to delve into it and satisfy your curiosity.

YOUR HEALTH: Physically, your stomach is your weak point and your liking for sweets and condiments endangers your digestion. The fluids of your body are more easily affected than is true with other signs. Being so susceptible to your associates and surroundings makes it easy for you to contract disease.

Because you are very nervous, little things upset you easily, so that worry may be a cause for ill health. Sickness in childhood may give you a delicate physique but strength may come with maturity. Care to avoid overindulgence can lead to a long life once your childhood is past. But your fondness for good food and all sorts of rich dishes may make it difficult for you to protect your digestive system by maintaining a strict diet.

Moods play a large part in your general health. Worry, bitterness, fear and gloom will lower your resistance. You are frequently sorry for yourself and may imagine that you are sicker than you are. You are afraid of illness and any pain has a great effect on you. Through your imagination and tendency to exaggerate your symptoms, there is a danger of acquiring the very disease which you fear. You should try to control your fears.

Cancer-born people are seldom tall and are often inclined to put on weight, especially as they grow older. Their facial expressions are soft and dreamy and sometimes rather vague—a "moon-face." Their noses are small and often upturned, and they are lymphatic types.

Cancer-born people usually lead quiet and unassuming lives for, although you can be as energetic as anyone else, you may lack the drive to push yourself into prominence. It is rather easy for you to procrastinate. Although in a sense you are weak, you can, on the other hand, be courageous and undergo pain and a good deal of mental suffering when the protective side of your nature is aroused —especially in protecting your home and the welfare of your family.

YOUR WORK: Your chances of being successful in business are good because you are usually thrifty, shrewd, prudent and careful. You are more suited to intellectual work than physical work and would make an excellent welfare worker. Any job which brings you in contact with the public appeals to you, such as charity work. Anything that captures your interest will fill you with drive and energy, which is often surprising considering your natural timidity.

You can be an aggressive and creative leader although your attack is never a direct one. You chip away at a hard task with quiet tenacity. And you often win before the other fellow fully realizes what you are doing. Sometimes this takes a physical toll of you, for you may appear courageous and strong but really become almost a "nervous wreck."

It is surprising how successful you are in your work, considering the uncertainty and pitfalls which face one today and which you fundamentally fear. You set about your work quietly and accomplish what you have to do before most people realize you have even started.

Any work that helps others is ideal for you. Your liking for children indicates that you might make teaching an enjoyable and successful career. Intuition is a great help to you in business and often you make your most important decisions on the basis of feeling rather than reason. Your ability to judge values and analyze problems correctly gives you success in real estate, investments and the like.

The sea attracts you, and you are at home in a career pertaining to liquids. Commerce and trading attract you and you can also hold positions of authority handling groups of workers. Basically you are artistic, but the development of any such talent depends upon you and your environment. All your creative work, whether poetry, prose, music or painting, has emotional appeal and plenty of artistic style. Any of the arts which draw upon your emotions and imagination offer scope for your artistic urges.

You have a strong sense of duty and are loyal to your employer and handle his interests with care. You are good at taking over extra responsibilities when there is a need for special effort, as during a "rush" season.

Regardless of how much money and prestige is attached to your work, your first consideration should be whether or not you are temperamently suited to it. In the long run, you will profit most if your job provides adequate expression for your personality. If it is absorbing work, there is less risk of your daydreaming too much and wasting your fine talents.

MONEY: You are careful where money is concerned and, being very honest yourself, will not tolerate dishonesty in others. Your tastes are modest and you dislike extravagant display. You have a keen sense of values, a flair for making money, and the prudence to keep it. If you become wealthy, it will be through your search for security, but you generally find it in the end. You are often the one who is able to help others.

As you are the worrying type, money may cause you some concern. Since this may undermine your health, it is best to work towards security without depending upon it too much. Sometimes you feel that you are being over-indulgent, but the possession of material things gives you confidence—and that is a quality you badly need.

YOUR HOME: There is a strong domestic side to your nature. You are a home lover and are devoted to your family. Sometimes you are prejudiced against outsiders and allow the family and home to become the be-all and end-all of your existence. The home and garden mean the world to you and you may have a fear of change in any form.

Your love of the past and old things is very strong, and you are inclined to collect things and store them away. Your cupboards and kitchen are rarely empty. You are fond of travel but you must always have a home to return to.

You like a beautiful home and, when young, are fond of your parents and home surroundings. When you have your own home, you will go to a great deal of trouble to make it secure and comfortable. You like to decorate it "just so." Your home must appeal to the romantic side of your nature, for it is there that you want to find sympathy and love.

You like to entertain and have friends about you, so that you can mother them and your family to your heart's content. Guests to your home are always well fed and made comfortable, and your welcome is always sincere. You feel the most secure in your home, so that it brings out the best in your nature.

Cancer people often carry on some sort of business in their homes, as it is easier to have people come to you rather than for you to go to them. The inspirational side of your nature is strong and the creative work it favors may be developed in your home. For instance, you may be a free-lance writer or artist.

You will probably spend more time in your home than those people born under other signs. You are proud of your home and possessions, and relish compliments from those to whom you offer hospitality. You will never be happy without a cheerful, happy, domestic life and, although your home may not be modern, it will always be comfortable.

FRIENDSHIPS: You like to have many friends and your fickle nature causes you to "shop-and-change" quite often.

Your friends may think you are sensitive, retiring and un-assuming, but underneath you are dying to be given the opportunity to come to the fore and be noticed. If your friends overlook you, ignore or neglect you, you become moody and peevish.

Self-centeredness is behind many of your reactions and it holds you back, because your senses are so acute and your imagination so active that you are inclined to let any hurt or slight affect you more seriously than it should. Your confidence is undermined and your friends will not want to be worried by your troubles and fears. Try to think more of others. They have problems too.

You like to talk over the old days with your friends, for you have a good memory and never forget the friends you have made and the good times you have had together.

Your intuition tells you when you have found a real friend and, should you lose one, it is a great loss to you. You may idealize and spoil those you like, especially if they appeal to your romantic and imaginative nature. You will not forget any kindness they show you.

ROMANCE: Life is dull for you without romance. You are affectionate and loyal and can be self-sacrificing where love is concerned. But love is frequently a whim of the moment which you cannot even attempt to explain. There are times when you are more than usually susceptible to another's approach, according to your mood. You give the impression of being restless, changeable and fickle. But once you really fall for somebody, your imagination and feeling come into full play. Depending on whom you come in contact with, you may need to withdraw into your-self every now and then to regain confidence and so avoid a dominating or nagging attitude, which is brought on only by a feeling of insecurity. You are adaptable and per-sonalities exert a great influence upon you. You are inclined to be too impressionable.

Your loved one means everything to you, and you may have a hard time finding the one who can measure up to the ideal you have in mind, as your standards are high. Sometimes they are too high and you are hurt when she or he fails to live up to them. Although you cannot afford to make a mistake, perhaps you could be less critical. You are careful in finding your love, but once you do, your affection never fails. You may play "hard to get," but once the right one comes along, you are easy to keep.

You have a basically possessive nature and can be over-bearing and jealous. Sometimes your romance suffers, for you can be thin-skinned and worry over fancied slights. If you and your lover do not see eye to eye, you can be-come remarkably stubborn and determined. Nevertheless, you are very much influenced by those you love. You always want to please them.

MARRIAGE: This is an opportunity to settle down, for a home and family are very important to you. Home is a refuge in which you can escape from the confusion and strife of the outside world. A happy marriage and home life are everything to you, and you enjoy your family to the full. You realize that it means a complete, normal life for you, and you look forward to it.

While you look for romance in marriage, often the marriage you make may be on the convenience side because you want to feel anchored. Sometimes your love of change may disturb you emotionally, but your material instincts for marriage and a home offset this by taking up all your thought and energy.

THE CANCER HUSBAND is not an easy man to live with, despite his easygoing nature. He may love his home but he is passive, lazy and self-indulgent. He may marry for money or status or for any reason that will bring him domestic comfort and an established position. He often gets what he wants because he can be so agreeable when he chooses to be. He means to be devoted and his whole mind is wrapped up in his wife and family, but often he spoils his good intentions by interfering in the household routine. He is never satisfied and can always find something to criticize or complain about. He may tell his wife what to cook and how to clean and he may seem harder to please than other types. He may be possessive and difficult but he is usually faithful.

THE CANCER WIFE is naturally sympathetic and inclined towards marriage. She needs the protection which a husband will give her. If she lacks character, she will need the help and guidance of her husband. She may put her husband on a pedestal and, if he fails her, she will probably suffer emotional shock. She is able to offer her husband spiritual strength in return for his guidance in meeting life's problems. She is the sort of wife who mothers her husband just as she does her children. She should try to be a little more independent.

CHILDREN: The maternal side of your nature is very strong. Cancer women are very motherly and even the Cancer man has something maternal about him.

You are happy with a large family. Adequate support and thorough education of your children are very important to you. If you have many children, they may reflect your varying and quick-changing moods. Cancer women make excellent mothers and the protective instinct is strong in Cancer men.

You willingly shoulder your responsibilities and, although your children may seem a burden at times, you can give up pleasure in favor of duty to them. This brings its reward, for your children are devoted to you. You do your best by them.

Cancer children are extremely impressionable. Their imaginations are fertile and they hero-worship other children. Their parents should realize that they need emotional understanding and attention. They crave love although it may be difficult for them to be demonstrative. They may even enjoy punishment if it brings them into the limelight for a while.

By now you are well aware that there are good and bad aspects to everyone's character, and that we can react to them or rectify them to our benefit. If you are a good type of Cancerian, you may have the following characteristics:

POSITIVE QUALITIES: While still subject to extreme sensitiveness, if you are the stronger type, you are able to control your emotions. Although you are capable of deep and understanding sympathy, you express it somewhat judiciously.

You are able to develop the spiritual side of your nature by delving into the problems of the soul and the unknown. Your imagination is vivid and you can sense other people's feelings and thoughts easily and "feel" atmosphere readily.

Your love for your home often develops into patriotism. Your sense of tradition is generally strong. You are receptive to the new and attached to the old. You like both antiques and modern furniture. You are compassionate and tolerant, and your friends and family will find you tender, gentle and always ready to help. Your sense of humor is wonderfully dry and kindly, never vindictive. You are more positive, energetic and determined than the weaker type of Cancerian.

On the other hand, the lesser type of Cancerian may have these characteristics:

NEGATIVE QUALITIES: You may find life difficult to cope with and dislike putting forth the needed energy to do so. You are spineless and unable to make a positive effort in any direction. You should overcome your timidity by constructive efforts towards practical results. You are touchy about your softness and frequently develop an inferiority complex or cocksureness to overcome it. You seek security and something stable upon which to pin your hopes. Both you and the stronger type find your home with its background of protective love a necessity. You have a great love of the past and an exaggerated idea of the "good old days." You want to be sheltered and protected and given your own way, to be petted and never opposed. Your home offers safety and a haven from reality. You are too much of an escapist.

You have plenty of feeling but it may not have much depth. Your affection may never develop into true love so that you may live purely for sensation, ease and flattery.

You may drift along, worrying as you go, and become secretive. You tend to be overanxious about the future, but your lack of enterprise and indifferent attitude make you seek the easy way out. You are passive and lazy and have no plan for life. Once you realize this and pay less attention to sentimentalities and vanity, you will be on the right road.

Cancer compatible with Leo, Virgo, Scorpio, Pisces, Taurus, Gemini.

Incompatible with Libra, Capricorn, Aries.

Leo

CHARACTER ANALYSIS FOR PEOPLE BORN BETWEEN JULY 21—AUGUST 21

YOUR PERSONALITY has the rare combination of an aristocratic bearing with the ability to command respect and the capacity to love deeply. Some of you may rank with the leaders of the world. You are independent and forceful, with a great deal of self-assurance. You are the type to form the backbone of the country; you have a keen sense of stability and preservation.

You have noble qualities and are heroic and generous. There is no ill will in the Leo nature and nothing small or petty, either. You are kindhearted, and never do anything sordid or low, though you are outspoken when you have the opportunity to be.

You usually mature early and attack the problems of life with zest and enthusiasm. Leo is the sign of sports, entertainment and every kind of pleasure. Everything connected with Leo is large, fulsome and generous.

By nature you are authoritative and commanding. You want to be at the head of things, to become the boss, for you sense your importance as a leader and feel that you have exceptional organizing powers and ingenuity. This is correct, and you are certainly constructive and inventive.

You are frank, broad-minded and just. At the same time, you have fixed ideas and can be dogmatic about them and quite stubborn. You are usually high-strung and may have a quick temper on occasion. But, on the whole, you have a placid nature and your bad moods rarely last for long.

There is no doubt about your dramatic talents, for you are a born actor and showman. There is also a poetic side to your nature. You love beauty and splendor and any form of display.

Others soon realize that you are susceptible to flattery, and even when they "lay it on thick," you accept it as your due because you have a pretty good opinion of yourself. This does not mean that you are vain, but reveals your consciousness of your own superiority. You can be rather easily led through flattery but you can never be driven. At the same time, you resent people persistently asking you for something; in fact you openly dislike their making any demands on you.

You like to map out your own life irrespective of others. You may become frustrated waiting for other people to make a move, for you are to a certain extent dependent on what they do.

YOUR HEALTH: Your physique is sturdy and robust, and it needs to be, to stand the strains of the Leo temperament. You are inclined to overwork and take on jobs beyond your capacity. If there is a streak of dissipation in your nature, you may not take any notice of warnings and end up by having a nervous breakdown. You are naturally energetic and enthusiastic and have a tendency to be rather extreme about things.

You should take care of your heart and spine as they will most likely have to bear the brunt of any unrestraint. You are susceptible to heart disease, epilepsy and rheumatic fever. Your constitution is pretty strong, however, and you recover quickly from any illness. Whenever you do become ill, you may be a poor patient, for you are impatient and want to be up and about. Your courage is mental rather than physical, so you are rather easily alarmed about your health. But you do fight any attacks of ill health with confidence and assurance. You will stand up for your principles against any odds. And in the face of physical danger, you make a great effort to get over your fear.

You love life more than anyone else, and should take special precautions against accidents, and control all rash inclinations. You will probably be vigorous through old age, for your will to live helps to prolong your life. To increase your chances for longevity, you should be careful to avoid overindulgence in eating or drinking.

Leo women are often very attractive, with ample poise and vitality. Both sexes usually have a gracious bearing and good features, neither too large nor too small, with beautiful eyes. The figure is usually finely modeled and the whole demeanor gives the impression of good breeding. Often the lesser type lacks the fine features of the more noble Leo and may have a heavy, fleshy figure.

YOUR WORK: You are best suited to work where you have sole authority. You will do well in executive positions, for you have a natural command of any situation. You have the ability to give orders and you speak frankly and criticize freely, often to the point of giving offense. You simply cannot see any reason for withholding a frank opinion, whether good or bad. Although you run the risk of being overcritical, people working for you always respect you, do their best willingly, and really make an effort to please and serve you. Your love and understanding of life and people are instinctive and your natural leadership arises from your earnest wish to communicate it.

Your natural instinct is to seek the highest honors, the best job, the first place in everything. Very often it is rightfully yours, for you have a fine intellect and understand human problems. You are not the type of person who has to plod ahead in search of knowledge. Your actions usually stem from your heart instead of your head.

Pride plays a large part in your work, for you cannot bear to fail. You attack your work with the intention of succeeding. You never become pigeonholed, but naturally work up to the head of any organization to deal with large issues, and leave drudgery and detail to others. You dislike menial work and will shirk it unless it has to be done as an example to others.

You have a deep sense of responsibility toward what you do, but are not happy taking orders from anyone else. Again and again you will revolt against another's authority, especially when you think injustice is being done.

You may rise to the presidency of an industrial concern or of a bank. You work well where you meet the public and shine particularly in politics, for here there are many opportunities to exercise control.

Usually you are artistic and creative and the theater may prove a good choice, as you may find close contact with an audience satisfying. There are also openings for a person like you in the contact and sales branches of advertising. Whatever profession you choose will have to be dominant, original and somewhat sensational. Public relations or publicity would be ideal.

MONEY: You are by nature a lavish spender, although poverty frightens you. If hard times come, you can usually bear them and staunchly stand by your family. You are not a spendthrift, but you want money and have the intelligence and drive to get it. You often make your fortune early in life, and your earnings are usually large, so that there is always money available for you to play with. Making a great show of wealth bolsters your pride. However, you should take care that your extravagances do not get out of hand.

You may have a weakness for gambling and speculations, but they usually result in substantial profit for you. But you do have to be a little careful not to let your self-assurance lead you to putting "all your eggs in one basket."

You could never refuse financial assistance if you felt it was really warranted, and you like to give expensive and lavish presents. Nothing pleases you more than to see others grateful for the gifts you buy them. You are always looking for ways to increase your prestige in their eyes. It is a comfort for you to know that others look to you for security.

YOUR HOME: Harmony in your home life is essential for your good health, as you need a place to relax. You like to be the leader in your home and have those about you absolutely dependent upon you for their well-being. You expect your family to uphold your proud standards in return for your devotion to them.

You are a good host and enjoy entertaining your many friends, but you like them to be of your own choosing and not of someone else's. You know how to make people welcome and feel that they are important to you.

You never stint yourself when it comes to spending money in order to have your environment, office or home reflect your power and glory. Your home will be an impressive one if you can afford it, and you usually can.

FRIENDSHIPS: You are popular and always have many friends. You make them naturally, and you generally have warm, firm relationships that continue for a lifetime.

Your ability to mix socially and get along with people is your greatest business asset. You always know many people who can help you up the ladder of success, although you may not be calculating in seeking them out.

Your friends will soon realize that you like to take the lead in any association. You must be the one to whom everyone looks up with pride and affection. Although you have the gift of mixing with the crowd, you like to remain a little aloof, for you feel that it is more dignified and fitting that you be like that.

ROMANCE: You can love deeply and, sometimes, not wisely but too well. Although you are conventional in most things, you are likely to be carried away by love. You are inclined to be sentimental and romantic at heart, with the chivalrous idea appealing to you. Not being flirtatious, you take your love affairs seriously and expect the object of your affections to reciprocate in the same way. You hate any demonstration of affection, especially in public, as you feel that such behavior is beneath your dignity and that you will lose respect. Nevertheless, you are very dependent upon affection, and you will be loyal to anyone you love.

You are attractive to the opposite sex, so that your loved one had better not be jealous. He or she will have to get used to your being the center of the crowd. Many women find the Leo man an ideal lover, for he can be fiery and passionate, compelling, masterful and very absorbing.

Sometimes, you make the wrong choice and are unhappy when things do not turn out for the best. Your pride makes it difficult for you to understand how anyone can deceive you or fail to respond to your affection. You like your romances to be gay, with plenty of parties and exciting times together. You should not let your romancing carry you away, for there is no halfway mark for you and you like to make the most of things.

MARRIAGE: Although you are conventional-minded in marriage, you give your whole heart and soul in your devotion. You are ardent and passionate and give yourself completely to your mate. If you do not receive the same sort of response from your mate, you may feel unloved and unsatisfied. Such unresponsiveness can do you much emotional damage, so your mate should learn to give as heartily as he or she receives.

You take the marriage vows very seriously, and once you promise to "love and cherish," you will do so with all your heart and energy. It takes you a long time to realize when you have made a mistake and you will do everything possible to live up to your marriage vows even when your mate proves unworthy.

Anyone who is fond of you will be wise to realize that you are not an easy person to live with, but there is compensation in your charm and affection. Someone who takes the trouble to understand and bear with you is well repaid.

THE LEO HUSBAND has no trouble fitting into the domestic routine. He wants his wife and family to be respected in the community and does all he can to provide them with what is necessary to do so. His own pride demands that he make his wife and family respected and socially prominent, to uphold his own position.

He likes, and expects, to be the center of attention and to have complete control of the household routine. Although he is loving and devoted, he will not tolerate any disrespect from family or servants. He has pretty fixed ideas about what is his due from his wife and family. He is deeply romantic and very absorbing, but feels his word is law and wants them to do only what he wants and considers right.

He has no scruples should he become involved in an outside affair, but if his wife behaved in a similar fashion, he would be horrified. She must be above suspicion and, as he is usually a keen judge of character, he usually selects a wife who meets his high standards.

The ideal wife for the Leo husband is the feminine, clinging type of woman. He will make a fine husband for her and she will appreciate his genuine nature and his kind and loving disposition.

THE LEO WIFE makes a fine mate. She loves intensely, is loyal and cooperative. She has a great deal of energy and is very capable; her appearance is always a credit to her husband. She may be an expensive luxury, for besides her extravagant tastes in dress, she expects a fine home with all the trimmings which will make an impression on others. To keep her happy, her husband will have to make an effort in this direction, but if he is not so inclined, she will spur him on. The family will have to get used to her fits of temper because she will not stop to reason with them but will act on the spur of the moment. Sometimes her basic pride turns into arrogance and conceit.

She is an ideal mate for the worldly, ambitious man.

She is most successful socially and can manage her home competently. She may hold prominent positions in outside interests and enjoys entertaining her husband's business contacts. She is the sort of wife he wants his boss to meet because of the favorable impression she makes.

The self-sacrificing Leo wife has a fervent and enduring love. She is sensitive, with a strongly emotional nature. She will lavish affection and attention on her family, for which they feel they can never show enough gratitude. Her devotion to her husband and family is so intense that she runs the risk of completely dominating them.

If she is lucky enough to marry a commanding man, she will exercise her authority to the right degree and will not overstep the mark. She will have the opportunity to exercise her housekeeping ability, lead the social group, and put all her faith and love into her relationship with her husband.

CHILDREN: You enjoy your home and are fond of children. And they will be naturally attracted to you. Children mean a great deal to you, but you should be careful not to assert your authority over them too much. Too much guidance and protection does not allow their own personalities to develop as freely as they should.

From an early age, Leo children show signs of leadership, and like to boss other children and monopolize the games they play together. They lead others—not into silly pranks—but as real little authorities who make themselves obeyed.

They love showing off and will do anything to be the main attraction. It requires great understanding on the part of the parents to gently make them take a back seat without damaging their self-confidence.

By now you are well aware that there are good and bad aspects to everyone's character, and that we can react to them or rectify them to our benefit. If you are a good type of Leo, you may have the following characteristics:

POSITIVE QUALITIES: You are probably endowed with more power than anyone else, using the word in the broadest sense. Physically, you usually have great vitality, and the same applies to your mental and emotional nature. You have considerable ambition and persistence and are very sure of yourself. These qualities combine with your generally effective personality, so that we find you occupying a position of prominence and authority, even though you may not have any special talent. If, in addition, you show real ability, you will go far.

The tendency to delegate work is strong in nearly all Leos, but if you are a good type, you will remain not a mere figurehead but a fine director who inspires others. In this respect the difference between the strong and lesser type of Leos is very easy to discern.

In thought and action you are positive and aggressive. Your mind could be called masculine; once you decide to do something, you will not hesitate to go ahead. You are usually certain that you have chosen the right course, but it might be wise sometimes to stop and reconsider it from other people's points of view. You may not always be right and should beware of dominating others.

On the other hand, the lesser type of Leo may have these characteristics:

NEGATIVE QUALITIES: Your greatest weakness is your arrogance. You may be thoroughly carried away by your opinion of yourself and your pride can make you very unpopular. You may develop into a snob who cannot say or do anything wrong.

You may bluster and bully your way in home life and business. Too often you are a pompous, self-centered showoff. You like blatant displays of generosity, and often there is a secret meanness beneath this. The outward appearance impresses you more than the merits of anything.

Although you are genial and often democratic in theory, in practice you are nearly always autocratic. Your powers of leadership have a detrimental effect. You try to win praise for yourself by appropriating what has been done by others.

Although you are temperamentally good-natured, obliging and often devotedly affectionate, these qualities are often ruined by the patronizing attitude you may develop towards others. You find it difficult to regard them as equals, which is irritating to those who do regard them as equals. However, a weak and clinging person will find this quality a source of strength and help; what may be in most respects a failing on your part will give a weaker personality courage and confidence.

Like most weak natures occupying high positions, you like to impress people. You like to be the focal point and are not likely to let others forget it. You may dramatize all you do and surround yourself with favorites who flatter you. Although you may promise the world, you often achieve very little. Your approach to life should be a little more realistic.

Leo compatible with Virgo, Libra, Sagittarius, Aries, Gemini, Cancer.

Incompatible with Scorpio, Aquarius, Taurus.

Virgo

CHARACTER ANALYSIS FOR PEOPLE BORN BETWEEN AUGUST 22—SEPTEMBER 22

THE KEYNOTE to your character is a practical mentality. There is nothing haphazard and superficial about you. You are painstakingly thorough, methodical and exact. In any situation, your first thought is for the most sensible and rational thing to do. Feeling never interferes with what you think is wise.

Your critical and discerning faculties are well developed, but you are secretly afraid of all that is great and over-powering. Instead, you are fond of all that is small. Nobody else can concentrate on minute detail with such diligence as you can.

You are a down-to-earth person and a perfectionist of the highest order. Your criticism often hurts, for you have the ability to "hit the nail on the head." It does not enter your head that you may be offending someone, and you should take care to be tactful in everything you do. Tact is not one of your natural qualities and it is difficult for you to develop it.

Good service is your aim in life and you set about it in an intelligent way. You do everything in a workmanlike fashion and are very skeptical of anything "unscientific." You learn easily but do not like to study. You are interested in all intellectual matters and like to have cultured people around you.

You could be described as a plain person with a clear mind who takes life placidly. You are not the idealistic, heroic or adventurous type, but you are trustworthy and decent. You are quiet and modest, very fashion-conscious and take great pride in your appearance.

Your thinking is along the lines of concrete, known facts and known quantities. You do not understand or credit flights of fancy or remote speculation. You analyze, dissect and study before arriving at a conclusion. You have not the slightest urge to investigate the mysteries of life and have no understanding of involved spiritual thought.

You are usually gifted with considerable artistic and literary taste; you do not lack appreciation of the simple things of life. But artistic endeavors are difficult for you because you cannot put the needed emotional expression into them.

As a rule, you are good-tempered and slow to anger, but when hurt by others, you are slow to forgive and capable of long-sustained resentment. You are not a fighter in the physical sense because you know it is more intelligent to arbitrate.

YOUR HEALTH: You usually enjoy surprisingly good health. Being a normally temperate person and knowing how to live sensibly, you will have a long life and healthy old age.

You are seldom ill although you often think you are. You may look for sympathy, but invariably do not deserve it. Ill health frightens you and you dramatize your illness whether it is real or imaginary.

Your weak points physically are your stomach and your nervous system, for both are very sensitive. You can aid your digestion by seeing that you have regular meals. You may become a chronic invalid and it will take quite a jolt to get your mind off an imagined illness.

You have a marked interest in matters pertaining to health, diet and hygiene. You usually watch your diet and are wise to leave highly seasoned food alone. You need plenty of rest and calm surroundings; also lots of exercise, which you may dislike.

You have a pleasant appearance, with a neat figure and small, precise features. Women born in Virgo are often beautiful in a somewhat empty, cold way. When you are young, you are very active and do not age quickly. Your youthful appearance stays with you throughout life although you may put on fat in later years.

YOUR WORK: You are dedicated to your work and proud of it. You like it and are often exceptionally industrious. You even like routine work and are the sort to stay in the same position for a long time. You can make great sacrifices for the sake of an ideal or aim and expect your work to show your ability. You have a deferential nature and do not stir up antagonism with superiors.

The right kind of work is important if your mind is to develop along the proper course. You may have many ups and downs in your struggle for security, but you will come out on top through effort and hard work. You will exert yourself if you can see how it will pay. You have many ideas and you try to perfect them all. You have ample reserve energy and you work quickly, though your attention to detail may make you seem slow.

You are capable of overcoming all sorts of handicaps and are not afraid to take on quite menial tasks if you feel you should. Sometimes, this might rob you of inspiration and take a toll of your health. Any work connected with detail, analysis, criticism and discrimination is suitable for you.

You may be a bookkeeper, accountant, teacher, doctor, pharmacist or lawyer. The good Virgo type is ideally suited to be a scientist. Great authors, journalists and poets have been born under this sign. You are suited to critical work of any sort.

An ideal partner for you in business would be someone with enthusiasm and courage, who will balance your qualities. You are inclined to worry too much about business affairs. Your methods are very detailed, so that you really need a partner who tends to use short-cut methods. Your diligence, trustworthiness and competence make you a great asset in any business partnership.

You may possess skill in manual craftsmanship and, either as a living or a hobby, become involved in work such as carving, metalwork or carpentry. You are fond of gardening or farming, but are also interested in science and abstract matters.

As a rule, you like to be left alone to carry out your job in peace and quiet. You make an excellent secretary or subordinate of any kind, as you dislike responsibility on a large scale. You do not often assume complete control of any concern and you shrink from the limelight.

You may become a slave to your work and you measure those who work for you by the same standards. You can be a hard taskmaster. People are not envious of you as you progress because your personality is generally insignificant. You do not inspire dislike or anger in others.

MONEY: Money may cause you some concern, but as a rule you are careful about money matters, for you possess a sound commercial instinct. You are conscious of the value of money and are always looking for ways to become rich. You are not lucky in investments because, more often than not, you let wishful thinking take the place of thorough investigation.

In your efforts to gain wealth, you should look out for dishonest deals. It is safer to learn to keep what you have. If you are persistent, you usually end up with security and comfort. You are a generous if not lavish spender. You are more interested in spending for the necessities of life than for pleasures or luxuries.

You do not usually come by great wealth and you may work hard without getting much in return, but your interest in a wide variety of subjects may nevertheless make you happy.

YOUR HOME: You like to entertain in your home, but must have everything perfect to be happy doing it. Both your guests and you and your family must be on their best behavior if a party is to be a success as far as you are concerned. You do not insist upon being the boss in your home but you do like everything to be shipshape, a place for everything and everything in its place. You safeguard your home and are careful to protect it from material disaster.

You are easy to get along with as long as you do not have to live in an upsetting atmosphere. Inharmonious conditions can have a bad effect on your health. Your lack of show or pretentiousness is evident in your home. In all matters, you prefer to judge and be judged on results.

You may have many changes in your home and in your environment. Wanderlust is strong in your nature. You always like a change in scenery, whether it be your home, your job or both.

You are often an excellent cook but may be a faddist in regard to food and correct eating. Your home is always spotless for everything seems to remain new.

FRIENDSHIPS: You are discriminating in your choice of friends and are often shy and retiring, making few friends. You are quite particular about whom you meet socially and you admire people who are intelligent, progressive and know where they are going. You are a good friend and are always ready to help, but you like your friendship to be appreciated. A person should never forget to thank you for a favor or any kind of friendly action. You like it still better if they repeat their thanks.

In meeting people you sometimes make the mistake of overrating intelligence. If someone appears sensible to you, that will override any adverse qualities they may have. Also, your fondness for all that is small can mislead you into belittling the personalities as well as the actions of your friends.

But it is difficult for you to be alone. You need people around you and, most of all, you need recognition. You usually lack initiative and need a push from your friends. Left alone, you feel frustrated, deserted and helpless. You need someone to bother about you and worry over you.

ROMANCE: You are naturally inhibited and your practical and service-giving qualities do not make for a romantic nature or glamorous love affairs. But the mere fact that you seem so indifferent to the opposite sex can bring you many opportunities for affairs. But when you are flirtatious, it is only because you enjoy the thrill of fencing with new contacts.

You may easily be dominated by one who has won your love, so it is important that you make the right choice. You will probably have a hard time finding someone who will measure up to your ideal of a suitable partner, as everything must be perfect as far as you are concerned. In some respects, you are a good deal of a shopper for love. Your idealism in love may cause you disappointment in early romance and you would be wise to be less intent on what you want to find in a person.

You do not readily admit that you need romance, as you like to think intellect comes first. And when you do find someone, your attitude is likely to be protective rather than romantic. You are very intent upon what is good for your loved one rather than what may be merely pleasant.

You are undemonstrative in affection, as you seem to be ashamed of emotion and even have a guilty feeling about it. You can be very reserved and introspective, and you dislike to have anyone prying into your private life. You really are very affectionate and are capable of great love, so you can afford to relax a little and not be so touchy about what is, after all, a very normal and necessary emotion.

You are basically the companionable type, so that you have to like a person well before you fall in love. Your romantic partners usually have the same background as yours. You forget that love demands understanding and cannot stand criticism. It can bring you a happy, full life if you will let it. Women born in Virgo are rarely passionate, and do not allow their emotions to run away with them.

MARRIAGE: You think it is sensible to be happy and practical to marry. You go about it in the right way and are a faithful mate. To some, you would appear cold and lacking in understanding but, if you marry someone with a similar intellect, it will be a delightful association. You are loyal and adaptable and make a good partner. You hate discord and will even stay married to avoid it. You are a kind, cooperative mate, suited to domesticity.

On the other hand, your married life may be unsettled and not too happy if you do not get just the right person.

As a lover, you are attentive and engaging but, as a husband or wife, you may be uninspiring. You may be so fussy and critical that you find it hard to make a decision about marriage. Frequently you do not make one at all and may remain a bachelor or spinster. This tendency to be too discriminating may cause you to miss out on many things in life. It is difficult for you to surrender yourself and you do not know how to give unrestrainedly.

THE VIRGO HUSBAND is not interested in love in the passionate, personal sense of the word. He is not usually very virile. He may have little male dominance in his make-up and he is as unlikely to demand surrender as he is to give himself. He has no passionate urges, and his deepest approach to love is flirtation or a play at love. He is not usually enthusiastic about serious love-making.

He is usually a conventional, tradition-minded man who accepts domesticity because it is part of the social scheme. He is willing to conduct his private life on a partnership basis, as if it were a commercial enterprise. More often than not he prefers to be a bachelor. He is abstemious and cannot bear to indulge himself. There may be a streak of stinginess in his nature.

He is a capable man making comfortable provision

for his wife and family. The material needs of his family are important to him and he will make every effort to provide the necessities of life, but may forget that pleasures and little luxuries are also needed. He may be overly critical and too prone to give advice. If he is peevish or complaining, especially about his health and expenses, he is also composed and thoughtful.

THE VIRGO WIFE is ideal in certain respects. Her idea of marriage is the legal partnership approach; it is to be carried out as smoothly as possible and in a business-like way. Her housekeeping routine may be perfect, for she is very efficient and her home is run like a well-regulated machine. There is no such thing as waste or neglect in her home, for she is always on the job.

However, sometimes the disposition of the Virgo wife is not good. She may find routine a strain and is apt to be nagging and meticulous in regard to material matters. She guards the family purse zealously and, in extreme cases, she is mean and oversees the running of the house like a fox. She is too prone to be critical over small things and may become faultfinding.

She responds to all the routine of life and meets duty extremely well. But she seldom offers spiritual companionship and emotional joy. She has in her make-up a selfish coldness that resents demands for more personal warmth. If she has these qualities, she is reluctant to share them. She may cling to the belief that sex is base, but a clever man who is in love with her might alter this frame of mind. Her best hope is for a man who is as restrained as herself, for in such company she will be most successful.

CHILDREN: Although you may appear to lack any maternal or paternal nature, if you have children you make a fine parent. You will train them in common sense and duty and in healthy daily routine. You love children but may be a little too strict with them. They have their own place and you firmly believe they must stay in it, and you put this belief into practice. You always do what is best for them so you may not give them much fun.

Virgo children have a tendency to fuss over little things and to worry unnecessarily. They may lack organization in what they do and need to be taught early to discern between what is important and what is unimportant. Their tendency to ask questions should not be discouraged, and as complete an education as possible should be given them.

By now you are well aware that there are good and bad aspects to everyone's character, and that we can react to them or rectify them to our benefit. If you are a good type of Virgo, you may have the following characteristics:

POSITIVE QUALITIES: Your steady qualities inspire admiration and respect from all those with whom you come in contact. Your abilities are suited to everything that requires conscientiousness, rational thinking, analytical ability and keen mental power.

You accomplish whatever you set out to do because you stick to your job no matter how long it takes or how tiresome it is. You often go further than many people expect through your patience and willingness to handle details. You are ingenious and humbly advance towards success through hard work and intelligent effort.

If you are this type, you lay the basis for peace in the world, for you dislike discord, and in your own manner endeavor to maintain harmony. In this way, you are a valuable member of society, for your contribution is by no means small.

Although you are critical of the faults of others, it usually stems from a desire to be helpful. You have an instinctive knowledge of what is good for people, and in a quiet way want to serve them by giving them this knowledge.

On the other hand, the lesser type of Virgo may have these characteristics:

NEGATIVE QUALITIES: You are cautious to the point of timidity. Although you may offer criticism in a sincere spirit, it may become sharp when you use it cunningly. Although your own tongue may hurt others, you hate to be scolded. Sometimes, your wit is not funny at all but cold and ironical. Some people resent such criticism so that you lose friends quite easily. No one likes to have his faults pointed out to him. You become angry easily and say cutting words, and you are bitter and unforgiving when hurt.

Your most common failing is to be too critical and discriminating, especially regarding details. You may be prejudiced and narrow in your views, with the result that you are unpopular with all who misunderstand your nature. Your love of methods also leads to fussiness and immersion in details, with a tendency to split hairs and become tedious and boring to the point of exasperation.

You can be priggish, for you are very moral and like to be admired for it. Your refinement may develop into prudery and a lack of charity toward the lapses of warmer-blooded people. You are too critical of what you consider to be sinful and you often fall victim to presumption, arrogance and gossip. Your greatest weakness is hypocrisy, but you are normal in your own demands and may suffer inner conflict as a result.

You are pedantic and often have an exaggerated love of cleanliness. You always know where everything is and cannot bear to have anything be out of order or untidy. You are so busy keeping small matters in order that you often miss what is really important.

If you attain a high position, you may be snobbish, with an exaggerated idea of what you have accomplished. You seldom discuss your thoughts and actions with others, for you value your privacy too highly.

You should do all you can to avoid self-pity, as it increases your tendency to be overly critical and faultfinding.

Virgo compatible with Libra, Scorpio, Capricorn, Taurus, Cancer, Leo.

Incompatible with Sagittarius, Gemini, Pisces.

Libra

CHARACTER ANALYSIS FOR PEOPLE BORN BETWEEN SEPTEMBER 23—OCTOBER 22

YOUR OUTSTANDING characteristics are love of harmony and justice and sympathy for pain and suffering. Equability and equanimity are distinguishing features in your make-up. Your keenest instincts are to weigh, measure and balance. You can see both sides of a question, understand the pros and cons, and finally reach a decision that is just to all. You seldom do anything without due regard for the consequences. Taking time to make up your mind often gives people the false impression that you are wavering when, in fact, you are merely making sure that you are acting without prejudice. In doing what you think is fair, you may even slight your own good.

Equilibrium is probably the most important word in describing your character. You make every effort to keep all things in balance and have great ability to compose disturbances and smooth out discord. You are temperate, intellectual, analytical and harmonious.

You are sociable, charming and companionable, and seldom lead a solitary life, as associations are most important to you. You are usually found doing your best work and achieving the most happiness when associated with others, either in marriage or in some other form of partnership. You have a talent for getting along with people, as you are affable, courteous and rarely guilty of wanting to injure others. You have an even temper, and when you become ruffled, get over it quickly. You seldom bear any malice; in fact, your temper is inclined to be short, and there is always a readiness on your part to forgive and forget.

There is much sweetness in your kind nature, and you can generally respond to better things when the opportunity arises. You are not wishy-washy, and beneath your serene and amiable demeanor, you have the necessary strength to protect yourself and to get what you go after. You are adept at the subtle approach and can influence others before they realize what you are trying to do. You often gain what you want through logic and your powers of persuasion. It is very difficult to deceive you.

All matters pertaining to art, beauty and elegance come within your sphere, as you have a highly developed sense of beauty which, after all, is usually dependent upon harmony. Often you long to escape from worldly conditions, and you suffer a great deal of secret unhappiness when faced with the roughness and hardness of life. You cannot stand what is vulgar or uncouth.

YOUR HEALTH: Your general constitution is usually good, but you can be rather easily thrown off balance in matters of health. You do not have much resistance to ill health but respond quickly to treatment. Your temperate nature and instinct for moderation do much to keep you in good health.

Your kidneys, spine and loins are the parts of your anatomy which should be guarded against ill health. You should not allow your system to become depleted or abuse natural laws. You usually know that you do not have much vitality and you are inclined to be more careful than others to avoid strain. Although you do not appear as strong as people born under other signs, you often outlive them.

You usually have a refined, elegant appearance, with a delicate, medium-sized graceful figure, regular features and small hands and feet. Everything about you—hair, eyes and complexion—appears well cared for and in good health.

Libra women are known to be the most beautiful in the

world. They have sex appeal, fine features, warmth of expression and soft, musical voices.

YOUR WORK: In your work you are quiet, pleasant, flexible and sensitive, but you are susceptible to your surroundings to such an extent that you sometimes will not move until you have found out what the other man is going to do. Your methods may be ingenious and shrewd, but you are not the enterprising type. You are not fond of the cutthroat competition of commercial business affairs and are more likely to be in the professions or in financial circles.

You are not fond of rough, ugly or dirty conditions and do not care to expose yourself to the more sordid aspects of life, so you are ill-fitted for work that involves unpleasant associations. Discordant or unclean surroundings will disturb your work and can even affect your health.

You are best fitted for partnerships of any kind. People learn to look to you to make decisions, for you excel in matters of judgment, analysis and instinctive reasoning. You may seem conservative, but this stems from an innate desire to be safe and to protect the other person against losses that might result from the untried. You do and say just the right thing at the right moment.

You have a high intellect and can understand anything up to the most involved philosophical argument. You can analyze, explain and pass judgment on all sorts of difficulties, with complete detachment. You do not allow your own wishes or beliefs to intrude. If you belong to the higher type of Libra, you are ideally suited for law or diplomatic work.

You may have a well-balanced temperament and naturally take a calm, dispassionate view of things. You always see things in their proper perspective. That is why your mind is invaluable in the legal profession and why many of you become attorneys and magistrates. You also make an admirable critic, because you have the power to put forward your opinions in a charming and amiable way. Suitable occupations also include those connected with liquids. You might do well as a chemist or as a hydroelectric engineer or be in the navy.

You should respond to your inspirational urges whenever possible. You should work on all creative material that interests you: stories, plays, music, paintings or designs. You should try to make your creative ability count, for without direction your inspirations may degenerate. You can rather easily become a dabbler.

There is an artistic note about most Librans; some of you rank with the world's greatest artists. There is thus available to you a whole range of occupational careers. Your fine ear for music and adaptability may combine to give you a talent for dancing.

You may make a good salesman, for your powers of persuasion can be irresistible. You sell with so much charm that others invariably buy more than they want. Modeling clothes is a suitable job for the sophisticated female Libran.

MONEY: You are not the type of person who concentrates on making money and piling up wealth. You are more interested in using it to satisfy your desire for luxury and beautiful things. Much money may pass through your hands but you may not retain it too long, as you are generous and your social leanings can prove expensive.

You like the things that money brings and are fond of display and elegant surroundings. It is easy for you to be extravagant because your idea of what is necessary can be very different from that of most people. You are not the saving type.

Although you may be easygoing and seldom thrifty, you are often remarkably shrewd about money. You have a great mathematical ability, and when you have to deal with financial matters can be surprisingly accurate. Financially you will not allow yourself to be imposed upon and often you resort to strategic plans to defeat attempts to fleece you.

YOUR HOME: Your home will always be charming and your family life harmonious. You have the taste and ability to select beautiful things. House furnishings, decorations and designs are all of a high standard in your home and you do well in professions related to decorating.

Your charming manner and ability to do things subtly without disturbance make it possible for you to get on very well in your home. But you do not have the strong, deep-rooted attachment for your home which some of the other signs display. You do not possess a strong domestic sense although any break with your family is very rare.

FRIENDSHIPS: You will probably have much to do with people, leading a fairly public life which will give you the opportunity to make many friends. Courtesy and honesty combined with a sense of justice make you an admirable friend even if you are sometimes unreliable. You respond to cooperation and are not happy as a "lone wolf."

Socially you are always in great demand. Your main desire is to avoid hurting the feelings of others. Although rather quick to anger, you are equally quick to forgive. Your conversation flows easily and you always give the impression of being well-bred. Even though you may have different inner feelings, society always believes you to be cool and unruffled. You do not ever say or do anything to interrupt the harmony of an occasion.

ROMANCE: One of the most interesting love natures of all is found in Librans of either sex. You are an expert on all matters pertaining to love. And, although you have great mental detachment, you are a most passionate person. Behind your poised front there is a physical nature very much alive. You are affectionate and considerate, and make a gentle, tender lover.

You are fond of company, particularly when it is pleasant, and you are likely to vary your interests and have many romances. You are frequently fickle and unstable in your affections. Your passion is likely to burn red-hot and then die out quickly.

You are highly susceptible and enjoy immensely the society of the opposite sex. Although you may be quite voluptuous, you are refined to a high point and your affairs usually have an artistic touch. You can be very sentimental and there is much in your make-up which appeals to a companion. You have a charming temperament, and although you are not constant in your devotion, your changes of affection are always tactfully handled.

MARRIAGE: Domestically, you Libra men and women fit into the scheme of marriage very well. You usually marry early in life and under all circumstances do all you can to preserve your home and are traditionally conventional.

Although you seldom seek divorce, you do like change. You are as gracious in your home as you are in your social life, but you are often a difficult partner to live up to. Your behavior is so near the ideal in outward human contact that your marriage partner has a hard time living up to your standards. The partner you choose may be a wonderful person, but entirely without your ability to adjust smoothly to the pace of life.

THE LIBRA HUSBAND is not an easy man to please. Domesticity is not really to his liking, but he is a passionate man and respects tradition, so marriage is the reasonable result. He is cheerful and compassionate and leads an ordered and wise life. His ability to guide the home is one of his greatest assets. He provides well for his family and seems to feel with the intensity of a woman the necessity for elegance and luxury in the home surroundings.

Love is a high art to the Libra husband. His attitude toward love differs from that of most men. His passion can be somewhat overwhelming and he rises to great heights in the expression of his love. If he does not get the type of response he needs and expects, he is deeply disappointed. Even when he finds his partner agreeable, he might be tempted to seek variety, but this is merely variety of expression. It is only when he is completely unable to adjust himself to marriage that he resorts to divorce.

THE LIBRA WIFE is a fine mental companion, wise in the way of partnership and able to bring, and maintain, harmony in her home life. In fact, one of her special gifts is her talent for harmony. She has an instinctive knowledge of how to get along with people and attracts an interesting social circle. At the same time, she never neglects her own family, but gives them all the loving attention of which she is capable.

She is quite definitely a luxury. She is usually very attractive and always has a group of admirers seeking her favors. While she requires a varied social life, she is too well balanced to encourage indiscriminate flirtation. But if or when she does find herself emotionally involved, her response will not be underhanded. She does not encourage scandal. Her existence is more complicated than that of a plainer woman, but her husband may feel confident that she will rise to the occasion.

She is the type who makes a lovely, sheltered wife. Her passions are voluptuous and she is responsive, intuitive and intellectual. Her response to married life is extremely satisfying. In many ways she is the best suited of all types to be the most desired wife in the strictly personal sense of the word.

CHILDREN: You make one of the best parents of any of the signs because you understand children and treat them with justice and gentleness. You are not likely to spoil your children and will be able to choose the best career for them and help them to prepare for it. You will not be tyrannical, but will guide and advise your children and be a companion to them.

Although you may not have a large family, you will enjoy your children and get much pleasure from playing with them. They will be a credit to you and of much help in your old age. They will be attracted to your charm, so that you can generally get them to do what you want them to do.

Children born under Libra need to be taught to use their will power and to have a definite purpose in life. They have a tendency to let things slide and can become lazy if they are not made to keep steadily at an endeavor until it is completed. At the same time, their creative ability should be encouraged, and they should be given an opportunity to express themselves through any artistic bent that appears. With a little guidance and firmness in harmonious surroundings, they will develop in an interesting way.

By now you are well aware that there are good and bad aspects to everyone's character, and that we can react to them or rectify them to our benefit.

If you are a strong Libra, you may have the following characteristics:

POSITIVE QUALITIES: Your impartiality, your sense of justice and your desire for fair play underlie many of your activities. You know how to use your quiet charm to get what you want without creating discord or making people angry. You are renowned for your diplomacy, and people find it difficult to quarrel with you.

You see other people's points of view and will always gladly adopt them if they suit you. You are rarely extreme in your views and can see both sides to a question. Therefore, you are valuable as a go-between who is always working to establish harmonious relationships.

Often you are much too polite to say "No" but prefer to say "Yes" until you are out of earshot. People are impressed by the noble gentleness and the sense of balance which you often convey. But underneath the apparent softness you have the firmness to succeed in life.

On the other hand, the lesser type of Libran may have these characteristics:

NEGATIVE QUALITIES: Your faults are weakness and compliancy. You find it hard to take a firm attitude in hostile circumstances, and you would rather avoid unpleasantness at all costs. You may compromise too much and waver from one view to another without giving a firm reply which commits you.

You may be spineless, lacking direction and purpose. You are always judging one course against another, trying to decide which is best, and, therefore, waste your strength in hesitation.

Often you are a moody person who exaggerates freely and likes to hear yourself talk. You can be very "sweet" but sometimes it is a sickly type of sweetness. In spite of your usual tact, you may deliberately ruffle the composure of others for the sheer delight of being able to compose differences and effect compromises.

Weak Libra people do not have the power to guide their families that the strong Librans have. You may be suave but lack the high intellectual development of which the higher type Libran is capable.

You may be shallow or insincere because you give way or compromise rather than face prolonged discord. You find a disturbed or quarrelsome atmosphere very hard to take as it may interfere with your ease and comfort.

There are times when you may deliberately lie, misrepresent and deceive. You can be slovenly and lazy when it suits you and refuse to act on your own responsibility, but instinctively seek a partner. You should take care that your life is not frittered away in self-indulgence.

Libra compatible with Scorpio, Sagittarius, Aquarius, Gemini, Leo and Virgo.
Incompatible with Capricorn, Aries and Cancer.

Scorpio

CHARACTER ANALYSIS
FOR PEOPLE BORN BETWEEN
OCTOBER 23—NOVEMBER 22

YOU ARE an extremist in every way. Of all the types, you are the most dominant, ruthless, self-willed and autocratic. You have a strong personality and, although you may be disliked, you are never ignored. You make it your business to see that this does not happen. You can be passionate and rebellious in opposing anything that does not suit your purpose. You will put forward your own claim before others, a hundred times if necessary, until you get exactly what you want.

In your nature we find the qualities that soldiers are made of. To you life is a battle and those who oppose you must be overcome. In doing this you are shrewd and crafty and usually get good results. You have great strength and energy and have an almost inhuman insensibility towards the natural feelings and reactions of others. According to your mood, all you can offer to the pain of others is biting sarcasm and scorn, or else an uneasy, disconcerting silence. It is very difficult for you to offer a few kind words of comfort; you seem to retire into yourself.

The puzzle to all who try to understand the Scorpio temperament is the combination of violent qualities and a fine, constructive mind. You have a far from shallow intellect and sometimes your thoughts are too deep to be expressed. Part of your existence seems to be spent in a world of your own making. You are philosophical, and the secrets of life and death and all that is unknown fascinate you. Your wits are sharp, and you generally remain calm and forceful under stress. You must have a constructive outlet for your energy, as you are not content to do things by half measures.

You can be contrary and contradictory in opposition, even to what you believe is right, if it suits your mood of the moment. You like to have things run in your own way, and you have an unswerving devotion to your principles. You understand life, its difficulties and problems, and are capable of deep sympathy and true understanding. With all your superior knowledge, you seldom take the easy way to accomplish things. You nearly always end up in an argument or strife of some sort, for you have a hot temper when aroused and provoke bitter dislikes and hatreds. Although you have a quick temper and sharp tongue, your angry outbursts do not last long.

Your speech is plain, blunt and sarcastic. You are very direct about most things, although you can be secretive about others. Your love of power is obvious and you will hit hard and fearlessly to get it. Your usual habit is to lay most of your cards on the table, but you like to keep one item of importance undisclosed.

You will not hesitate to discard old habits, methods or acquaintances for the new and dramatic. Often these changes are drastic and surprising.

YOUR HEALTH: You have a strong, healthy body and certainly never pamper yourself. In fact, one of the important dangers to your health is neglect and abuse of your body. You move with effortless power and work with great energy. Scorpios are usually good at sports, so that you revel in strenuous exercises. You dislike giving in to sickness and have great powers of endurance. Your stamina and constitution enable you to stand up to great strain, and sheer will power often pulls you through any illness. Only when you are very ill do you give in. At this time you must temper your violent passions or they will have a serious effect.

Your intense nature renders you liable to breakdowns of all kinds. Sometimes you are unable to rest and relax, but can bear up to pressure when it is on. Your physical weaknesses are located in your digestive system, and you are prone to disregard minor disturbances until they become major illnesses. You are liable to catch infection easily, and any poison entering your system will weaken your constitution considerably. You must take care to prevent illness as well as to cope with it.

But when you are sick, you put all your energy into combatting it as you do in the other affairs of your life. You will probably go to bed and use the most powerful medicines at your disposal. You will also resort to surgery whenever possible as it appeals to your drastic nature and sense of the dramatic.

Both Scorpio men and women are likely to be sturdy and thick-set, with large bones. The male usually has a dark complexion, with a protruding jaw and determined mouth. The eyebrows may be bushy and the eyes deep-set and cold. Scorpio women tend to be voluptuous and husky-voiced, with oval faces and full mouths, possessing a beauty all their own. You seem old in youth and youthful in old age.

YOUR WORK: You are an industrious worker and always make a point of doing your job thoroughly. You have plenty of drive and are extremely temperamental in your work, which affects your output. You dislike physical labor, but are bent on achievement. You realize that you can help yourself through your work and are often very successful.

You usually have great ability, are highly accomplished and work with tireless energy. You are ambitious and progressive and are hardly ever found without work.

In the intellectual field, you are able to grasp and master any subject. You often take on jobs that others avoid, through sheer will power and the desire to make a success of them. You never give up and do not like things to get the better of you. Usually you succeed through thorough, systematic and capable work. You are not entirely selfish in your work and attitude. You will work for others, often long and thanklessly.

The desire to explore the unknown is strong in you. You work tirelessly in the medical field and are well fitted to carry out research. You are successful because you test everything precisely, keenly and without prejudice. Scorpios make excellent scientists, doctors, nurses, laboratory assistants and lawyers. You can also excel as detectives and investigators of all kinds.

You bring emotions into play as you come into contact with others. These emotions can range from worship to hatred, but never indifference. You will work on and get results, long after others have given up. If you head any project, others will accept your inflexible leadership and, though you may be hated, you will always be obeyed. Work carried out under your direction will always be well done, never second-rate.

In many ways you are a prolific and prodigious worker. You have great powers of concentration and are very efficient. There is often a streak of genius in your nature and you are extremely resourceful. In any job you take on you never compromise or take the middle path, for you are capable of the highest and finest. You can handle any emergency and never admit defeat. You do nothing by halves and, having selected your course in life, pursue it relentlessly. You have powers of leadership and, as an employer, you demand the maximum effort.

MONEY: You are lucky where money is concerned. Somewhere, somehow, you are always able to find it for whatever you want. Money is one of your chief goals in life and it is likely that you will eventually have a substantial income. It is the same in anything you think necessary—money, a car, a business or a family. Once your mind becomes set on a goal, you will pursue it relentlessly until you reach it. You waste no time in getting what you want and your achievements will be considerable.

You are as shrewd in handling money as you are in seeing through people and detecting their motives. However, you need to be careful not to spend money foolishly, as you are generally a liberal spender.

YOUR HOME: Although you are temperamentally unsuited to a well-ordered domestic life, environment can play a vital part in your success, and the love and understanding you find in your home are important. You are adaptable enough so that once you are settled in your home, you put all the management and energy of your passionate nature into your home. You like to be the boss in your home and always have the final say in any matter. Behind this is your feeling that no other decision is as good as your own.

You have a gift for making your home comfortable and even luxurious. Your house is generally tastefully designed, but may be more ostentatious than modest. You are proud of your wife and family and like to show them off in a setting you feel they warrant. It provides you with an outlet for your artistic and creative urge, which is very strong. Sometimes the flamboyant streak in your nature gets out of control.

FRIENDSHIPS: In all human relations Scorpio revolts. There is rarely a Scorpio man or woman without enemies. You love fighting, from a battle down to a quarrel, and it is your nature to divide and mix. But people are attracted to your magnetic personality and will find you reliable and genuine. You are very loyal, as a rule, to those friends you do make, but if anyone lets you down or hurts you deliberately, you can retaliate relentlessly. Unfortunately you sometimes hold a grudge.

You are a good friend, but when you feel a friendship is becoming too intimate, there will be friction. You seldom make lifelong friendships. Powerful and practical friends, influential people of property and office-holders come into your range of friends. Very often there is no solid basis for a long-range acquaintance.

Sometimes a parent or a superior may point out a weakness to you, which will bring on a critical time for all concerned. This may lead to a greater appreciation on your part, which can create more affection on both sides. As a Scorpio you make mistakes but are forgiven all through life, and anyone who gets close enough to understand your strange and contradictory nature may be your friend for life.

If you learn to control your violent nature, your chances of being more popular will increase and others will be more sympathetic towards your ups and downs. You are nearly always impossible in an argument, for only you can win. You should make the most of cultivating the brilliant friends and influential persons whom you have the opportunities to meet.

You are generally quiet and like to spend much time alone, although you also like society. It is not your nature to make a fleeting acquaintance or a light conversation, and your friends may find you deep and difficult to truly understand.

ROMANCE: You are as dynamic and intense in romance as you are in everything else you do. Love plays a vital part in your life, and to keep your life running smoothly you must have sympathy, understanding and affection. Your romances may have their trials. You thrive on compliments and appreciation from your loved one, but when criticized, you are moody and disagreeable. However, there is no limit to the trouble you take to make the object of your affection comfortable, happy and secure.

You have no time for light flirtations, for your emotions are intense. You need complete reciprocation in love. You are proud but have a warm and generous nature. You are passionate and inclined to be possessive and jealous of your loved one.

You take romance seriously and once you try to flirt, you are lost. Naturally enough you need love and are unhappy without it. You are prepared to give much for it. You like demonstrations of affection and are capable of an intense dislike of anything or anyone who comes between your love and you. You will stop at nothing to do away with the obstacle. Until you learn to be more restrained, you can be mistrustful, exacting and suspicious.

An ideal partner for you is one from a similar cultural level, with a character similar to yours—the same urges, feelings and interests. If you both have a common objective in mind, you will go far together.

MARRIAGE: A successful marriage is most likely when your partner is docile, yielding and subject to your complete guidance. You place great value on yourself and what you have to offer, and therefore demand a great deal from any partnership. In any association, you never quite give up all you have to offer and you generally have much to give. You are by nature faithful in marriage, but you are not content to sit at home and watch life pass by. You seldom want to break up your marriage once your true love is given, and you will work hard to improve anything inharmonious in the relationship.

THE SCORPIO HUSBAND has a deep and genuine affection for his wife and family, but he can be very selfish and stubborn. Often he is demanding, jealous and overbearing. He is one of the most difficult to live with in peace and harmony. This can be done if his wife is receptive to his thoughts and obediently follows what he tells her. He is difficult to take lightly when he is persistent about anything he wants. He is definite about being the head of the household and wants to be recognized as such. Sometimes he carries this to extremes and an unhappy marriage is inevitable.

There are more chances for happiness for the moderate Scorpio husband, who is often successful and well able to support a wife and a large family. Even so, his intense devotion and possessiveness are often a strain on his family. No matter how much love and attention he receives, he is often secretive and doubting and will twist things around in his mind to make them appear to be working against him. This is all in his imagination, but he persists in getting impatient and resentful.

THE SCORPIO WIFE takes marriage and all its responsibilities very much to heart. Although she may keep her family in a state of nervous exhaustion through her temperamental outbursts, she has an old-fashioned reverence for domestic duties. She is not dismayed when her husband unexpectedly brings home guests for dinner. She is usually a good cook and does not make an effort over her household tasks.

She puts her heart and soul into her love for her husband and family, but she does not idolize those she loves. Because she looks at life perhaps a little too realistically, she sees them as they really are. If her attitude changes and she falls out of love, then she will do what her heart tells her, often without fear of the consequences. She is rarely deceived and has no illusions, nor does she try to deceive herself, but accepts the facts in a clear and level-headed way.

CHILDREN: You like a large family even if you fall down in your parental responsibilities. You can be a severe parent although you have good intentions. It is very difficult for you to see the child's point of view and you expect your own wishes to be followed without any latitude. Your temperament may be unsuitable, as you can be tyrannical, possessive and even violent. Your devotion to your children may be genuine and your intentions may be good, but life for your children may be difficult and confusing. However, you almost always marry and have many children who will, in the long run, probably turn out well if you practice patience and understanding.

Scorpio children have a great deal of will power and are shrewd and difficult to deceive. Parents have to be very frank and straightforward with them. They have strong affections and great care should be taken in training them so that they are not ruined by overindulgence on the one hand, or harshness on the other. Although they are physically strong, their emotional natures need the most careful treatment.

They should be given every opportunity to work off their nervous energy or they may become impatient, contrary and difficult to handle. They can too easily become problem children when not understood. Insecurity and selfishness are the most common faults which parents have to try to rectify in their Scorpio children.

By now you are well aware that there are good and bad aspects to everyone's character, and that we can react to them and rectify them to our benefit.

If you are a good type of Scorpio, you may have the following characteristics:

POSITIVE QUALITIES: You are an indispensable part of humanity and are earnest and brave. You are generally very observant and proceed cautiously in spite of your fearlessness. You are decisive in word and action and are persevering and determined once you have set yourself a goal. Whatever you gain in life is earned through sheer hard work. You make straight for your objective without beating about the bush. You are combative and refuse to be sidetracked by misfortune.

Although you appear, on the surface, to be hard, deep inside there is great tenderness. You have profound and enduring feelings and, in a strong Scorpio, these become set and develop into an unwavering devotion to principle, deep sympathy and true understanding. You still maintain your strength of conviction and faith in yourself in the face of all opposition.

Often you have an urge to be self-indulgent, and powerful feelings constantly tempt you. Few Scorpios go through life without facing temptation. The strong type is able to develop self-control and self-denial. If you are of this strong type, you will be dignified and possess a sense of pride and self-respect.

Your manner and speech are generally restrained and grave and you do not readily unbend, even in society. You have a natural tendency towards what is secret and hidden and love probing mysteries and getting to the bottom of things.

NEGATIVE QUALITIES: You may have a sort of vicious strength and daring intensity and are capable of using cunning and cruelty. The deep feelings that are common to most Scorpios are more uncertain with you, and you may be given to bitter dislikes and hatreds which you may nurse for a lifetime. If you are this type, even though you may have to wait many years, eventually you will settle the account. The only reason for revenge is to get the person or condition out of your system.

You may be extremely sensitive to imagined slights or injustices. Often you think yourself victimized or undervalued and you may relieve your feelings through constant boasting. You may take a secret pleasure in being tricky, subtle and clever, and often disconcert others with blatant displays of knowledge. You often worry about things that never happen. Whatever good you achieve is colored by your own pessimistic temperament, even though your common sense and experience have taught you that the facts are different.

Often these negative qualities appear in childhood, but

die out with good training. In both types there are strong affections and the making of solid citizens and worthy friends.

Scorpio compatible with Sagittarius, Capricorn, Pisces, Cancer, Virgo and Libra.

Incompatible with Aquarius, Taurus, Leo.

Sagittarius

CHARACTER ANALYSIS FOR PEOPLE BORN BETWEEN NOVEMBER 23—DECEMBER 20

YOUR INTELLECT is of a very high standard and your outlook is mature, farseeing and imaginatively practical. You are quick to understand and willing to assimilate new ideas and ways of living. Most of your intuitive decisions are likely to be right, for your intuition is very strong. "Healthy and wise" is a good description of you. You lead an active out-of-doors life. You have wisdom but not necessarily many material possessions.

You are broadminded, tolerant, humorous and truthful. Your love of the truth can have unfortunate results, for you can make any statement simply because it happens to be true, but forget to take into consideration the effect this may have. The majority of people do not like hearing the truth about themselves, at least not as frankly as you put it.

Just as you tell others the truth, you expect the same from them. And even those who dislike you will admit that if everybody were like you, there would never be any serious arguments.

You are optimistic and confident and have a joy of living that others find infectious. You seem to have found your equilibrium physically, mentally and spiritually. You like variety, for you are fond of sports, studying and reading, while you still have time to enjoy the theater and the other performing arts. Religion also plays a strong part in your life.

Your sense of justice is one of your greatest assets. This might cause you to revolt, but your aim will be, not to bring about something new, but to re-establish law and order and to see that the oppressed gain their rightful claim. That is why you are so successful in legal positions, and you certainly make an excellent judge or lawyer.

The urge to travel is very strong in your make-up. You want to get away from everyone and you are attracted to faraway places. You do not like city life and, of all types, you are probably the one closest to nature. You love the country and animals, especially dogs and horses, and they love you. One can picture you as the farmer, or as the cheerful adventurer and globe-trotter.

The spirit of fun is strong in your nature, so that sometimes it is difficult for others to know when you are serious and when you are merely joking or teasing. "Many a truth is spoken in jest" can apply to many of your remarks. You like to argue and seem to have an uncanny knack for finding the weak points in your opponent's ideas. Your finely developed humor gives you the ability for swift and witty repartee.

YOUR HEALTH: Physically, Sagittarians are distinguished-looking people, being tall, well-developed and athletic. You have a contagious enthusiasm for anything you do and take an active interest in outdoor exercise. Physical activity is a "must" for you, and you seem to grow in strength and virility as life goes on. You rarely allow your regrets and worries to get the better of you, so that they do not generally contribute to ill health.

To be fit means a lot to you and your health is usually good. Your body is sound but your nervous system is delicate. Living so much on your nervous energy creates a danger of nervous exhaustion. You like to be on the go and often this results in overstrain from too much activity, both mental and physical. It is dangerous for your health if you scatter your energies in too many directions for, strong as you are, your nerves will have to sustain you. Sudden illness can come from exposure and risks, resulting in a loss of nervous energy. Your great love of sports and your frequent recklessness can lead to injuries.

Fevers may set in when you drive yourself to a peak of activity and continue to work long after another person would have recognized the signs of illness and given up. You have a great deal of reserve force which is helped by your ability to rest easily.

You may suffer from indigestion and, later in life, from high blood pressure, rheumatism and sciatica. Your hips and thighs are important parts of your body to be protected, especially against accidents. It may be that your love of life and your urge to see what happens in the world preserve you to old age. With care against overdoing, you can expect general good health and a long life.

Sagittarius women have a beauty of their own. They are graceful and unaffected. Their deportment is usually excellent, as they carry themselves proudly erect.

YOUR WORK: You are a loyal, energetic and capable worker. You are aggressive and progressive and like meeting challenges, so that you are excellent when working for a cause. However, you do not like taking orders or being confined to office routine. You like to work where you meet people and your work is likely to suffer when you have to stay in one place. You like frequent changes of employment, and those you associate with should give you a free hand if you are to produce your best.

If your work is not sufficiently occupying, you will branch out into outside interests without bothering very much about the consequences, so long as your interests are given an opportunity for expression. You aim high and get more pleasure out of hitting the mark than you do out of the rewards or acclaim you may earn.

You make a wonderful teacher, writer and journalist; you are also well equipped to be a lecturer or public speaker. There are many occupations in which you could be successful, for you are very versatile. Publishing, advertising, government work, office executive, foreign affairs and music are all fields that you might explore.

Your mental abilities also, as a rule, are above the average and, if you are a good type, you have a great interest in philosophy and religion. You may be a successful politician or clergyman, because you have qualities of vision, practical power and human sympathy.

You are pleasant to work for and with, for you have self-reliance and give confidence to others. You have a fondness for detail and many ideas, for your inquisitive mind is always seeking higher knowledge.

MONEY: You are a generous person, never mean or petty. You are almost invariably well off; but if you are ever broke, you are always hopeful, for you have a happy-go-lucky attitude. You are anxious to make your pile and will take risks in gambling, for you always feel lucky and, strangely enough, money seems to come to you naturally.

"Expansion" and "promotion" are key words in your character and you will embark on big projects readily if you feel you will benefit financially. Your intuition, which is so helpful in all the affairs of your life, will be doubly useful in money matters. But sometimes you refuse to follow it and may take chances that are too big.

You are intrigued by "get-rich-quick" schemes and are usually successful. You have a keen business sense and many opportunities will come your way. You would be wise to get all the training you can to make the most of these opportunities. Your greatest chance of making money will probably come later in life, through investments. You inherit little in the way of money, and whatever you achieve in the way of finance or position will be through your own efforts.

Happiness is more important to you than wealth or position, and you are quite prepared to lead a simple life as long as it is a free one. "Give and spend, and God will send," is an axiom which quite accurately describes your attitude towards money.

YOUR HOME: Your sense of the home is small and often outweighed by your other interests. The whole world interests you so that you find it hard to confine your thoughts and affections to your home. Your interests are too diffuse to enable you to be a success domestically.

You appreciate the simple things in life and your home will reflect this. Here you will need a certain amount of independence and you will insist upon it. You will not stay where you do not get it. You like a neat and orderly house where you can still have fun and enjoy life. You like to see beauty about you, but the work involved in keeping things looking well bores you and you become very restless.

You like children and, once you settle down, you will find great happiness. You like your friends around you and are fond of entertaining. And people like to visit you and be with you because you give them courage and optimism.

FRIENDSHIP: Your qualities for making friends are fine and they will probably be of all classes, for you like an assortment. You are likely to make friends on the impulse of the moment who develop into friends of years' standing. You are the type to take a lot from others, but you cannot be fooled by insincerity.

You are invariably well-liked, for you have a ready wit and smile, and people value your friendship. You have a keen sense of humor, which they appreciate, although you are generally serious and light chatter does not come easily to you.

Although you are never afraid to speak your mind freely, there is also an opposite side which sometimes makes its appearance when you are reticent, sensitive and impressionable. This could be called a smoke screen, for you are often hard to know because of this duality of your nature.

You are kind and understanding but, when you are with those who are hostile to your temperament, you may become irritable and impatient, or even defiant. Although you are normally gentle, you can become formidable when aroused.

ROMANCE: You have a sympathetic, affectionate nature which is not possessive, and you are very loyal to those you love. You do not value personal possessive love as highly as universal love, and your romances must bring you mental as well as physical satisfaction.

You may make a sudden attachment and pursue it diligently, but end it before reaching the altar. Once your feelings begin to cool you cannot be insincere in your promises at the ceremony. That is why you may have many romances before finding the right one. That is also the reason why there are so many bachelors among your sign.

Once you have found the right one, you are easy to win but not so easy to hold, for he or she may find it hard to keep up with your high-spirited and impulsive way of life. You regard your romances as adventurous outlets and escapes from reality.

Disappointments in love may come early in life for you because you are immature and act unwisely on occasion. Although you may have many romances, there is generally only one real love in your life. Your love is direct and positive and, when you finally choose a partner, you do it with deliberation. When those you love do not measure up to your high standards, you must realize that you will have to accept them as they are.

You have very high ideals which mean a lot to you, and you love your freedom. You realize that you can lose both in the course of everyday living so that you do all you can to preserve them. You avoid jealousy because you see in it a threat to your own freedom of action, which you prize so highly that you are willing to fight for it.

MARRIAGE: You do not like your freedom to be curtailed and are wary of a too domestic atmosphere. You like to do things with other people and are not happy with one who wants to sit at home all the time. You sometimes forget that you must try to understand the other person's viewpoint, and give a little, too.

You cannot tolerate being tied down and, even when you submit, you may become irritable and can be sarcastic. Your temper may flare up quickly but it is only for a short time. You require understanding and companionship. You need someone to turn to at all times, to whom you can tell your troubles. Your partner must enjoy your interests and hobbies or you will enjoy them on your own.

THE SAGITTARIAN HUSBAND is invariably a gifted man with whom it is a privilege to live, but because of his lack of the personal sense and his impatience with anything narrow or ordered, his wife must broaden her own outlook so that she can see eye to eye with him.

He requires a wise, tactful wife, for he has much to give if treated in the right way. But he is not ideally fitted by nature for a domestic life. His interests in outside affairs, his business and his sporting activities, all take much of his time. He loves humanity and is respected by and plays a prominent part in the community.

All his strength goes into life in general, so that his personal life becomes unimportant by comparison. Often his personal tastes change, for he is not hypocritical enough to continue to express his devotion when it does not exist. His wife should be broad-minded and quite impersonal if she is to hold his interest.

THE SAGITTARIAN WIFE is the best fitted of all types to be a companion to her husband. She takes an active interest in her husband's business affairs but does not intrude and waits until she is asked before offering her ideas or advice. Her good intuition and prophetic nature makes her advice usually worthwhile.

She is attracted by life in the open, to all kinds of activity, social life and intellectual advancement. It is easy to see that a husband can have a full life with such a companion. She is a competent wife—efficient, clever and well-balanced. She can be trusted, for her judgments are mature. She is rarely suspicious and is able to tactfully overlook her husband's preferences. On the other hand, she can be outspoken about her husband's or children's errors. This may be a good thing, for hers is generally a constructive criticism.

CHILDREN: You have not much time for children when they are small, for you feel clumsy and unable to look after them. Once their minds and their interest in sports develop, there is likely to be a strong bond between you. They are drawn to you because you love life and want to have fun with them more than most grownups do.

Sagittarian children are nervous and restless. They need mental exercise as well as physical. They start striking out for freedom while still very young. They will try to overcome any form of restriction and they show their independence at an early age.

Nothing is worse than for you to try to supervise them all the time. You should let them feel that you rely on them, and their sense of honor will be your best guarantee.

If they think that you do not trust them, you will lose their confidence, perhaps for good.

By now you are well aware that there are good and bad aspects to everyone's character, and that we can react to them or rectify them to our benefit. If you are a good type of Sagittarian, you may have the following characteristics:

POSITIVE QUALITIES: One of your strongest characteristics is your mental activity which you combine with physical activity in your attempts to reach your goal. To you, nothing seems impossible, and you aim for the highest goal. You are very idealistic but you have the ability to reason out every question. You face life optimistically and cheerfully, which attracts people to you. You have a prophetic nature, with the ability to see far ahead and to know how things will come out. You should rely on your intuition, as it is very strong.

You are a person of the highest integrity and morals: frank, free, sincere and honest. On the one hand, you are enterprising and daring; on the other, sensitive and retiring, but always pleasant and confident. You have the ability to become a leader of the church or state.

Maturity and success do not come early in life for you. Your distinguishing qualities—understanding of philosophy and religion, direction in life and decisive action—come naturally with age and experience. Your life is generally one of sincere service, and those you meet as you go through it will profit in many ways from your acquaintance.

On the other hand, the lesser type of Sagittarian may have these characteristics:

NEGATIVE QUALITIES: You may be lazy and boastful, but people still consider you a pretty decent individual. Inconsiderate behavior is one of your worst faults, and you can be very tactless at times. You can be both crude and rude on occasion, and may have the knack of saying that one little extra word that hurts.

Whenever your emotions are involved, you may become very talkative and it is likely that you will exaggerate. There is no limit to the variety of stories you can invent. You may promise the world in a weak moment, but may not have the slightest intention of keeping your promise. You like to flatter and always have an empty compliment to hand out.

Your exuberance may lead to extravagance, lack of concentration and carelessness over details. You are cocksure. You may give the impression of knowing a little about everything but not enough about any one subject.

You may be the sporty, gambling type of Sagittarian who is out for a good time and relies on your friends or family to protect you from the consequences of your actions. You may be an exhibitionist who develops a sudden craze for people, intellectual interests or hobbies, which works up to a pitch and then dies away. Despite your philosophical outlook, of which you are very proud, you have many prejudices and even hatreds.

Sagittarius compatible with Capricorn, Aquarius, Aries, Leo, Libra, Scorpio.
Incompatible with Pisces, Gemini, Virgo.

Capricorn

CHARACTER ANALYSIS FOR PEOPLE BORN BETWEEN DECEMBER 21—JANUARY 19

You ARE ambitious, strong-willed and definite in purpose. Your life is governed by these qualities and all your actions are directed to this end. Once you put your mind to it, there is almost nothing you cannot do. You are always striving for something higher and you throw your whole heart and soul into whatever you take on. Like the goat, you climb doggedly, using everything and everyone that you meet on the way up. Others, in turn, profit from their contact with you, for you inspire confidence and clearly appreciate their values which you lack. You are never satisfied and will work for something better, in your own shrewd way. You are constantly seeking perfection. You are constantly looking for the ideal in life.

Your outstanding characteristics are loyalty to anyone and anything you consider worthy of it, and devotion to whatever you take on. You have charm and are dignified and reserved. In fact, you find it difficult to take a joke and really have a good laugh about yourself. Life is real to you and you realize that struggle is needed and that time should not be wasted. Criticism is hard for you to take at any time, even though it may be well meant and comes from someone you love.

If you are a strong Capricornian, you have a fine mind—slow but capable of deep concentration. You are conscientious and exacting and take pride and care over whatever you do.

You are just, placing more emphasis on justice than mercy, and you are not soft or unselfish. Sometimes you are even pitiless. You cannot bear weakness or indecision. You are intellectual, a good organizer, and have a strong sense of honor.

If you are a weak Capricornian, your faults are worldliness, snobbishness and a sense of inadequacy. You are insecure and become depressed. This overrides the practical abilities you have. You are unable to find a place in the world and you turn from one thing to another, from one job to another. You may be clever but ineffectual, and you seem to be looking for something you will never find. Your mental outlook may become narrow; your respect for the past pulls you back and you refuse to progress and change with the times. You will always use others for your own ends, and you often put your own personal advantage uppermost. You become full of your own self-importance; you are afraid of being overlooked by others.

You are a very conservative person and are not likely to do anything to upset existing conditions. To a great extent you rely on past authority and methods which are tried-and-true. You are not the sort to set new standards or to seek to change the boundaries of your environment; it is easier for you to work within it. You like to know exactly where you stand.

YOUR HEALTH: You generally get off to a poor start in life, but as an adult you become strong, with great powers of endurance. It is your nature to fight defeat and you need a great store of energy for this. You are very active and have an excellent chance of leading a long life. The bones and joints, particularly the knees, of a Capricornian are most susceptible to injury. You may suffer a lack of calcium, affecting the teeth. Skin troubles may be frequent and, later, rheumatism and arthritis. You generally have a practical background and eat wisely in your youth. This, combined with hard work and a planned future, probably accounts for your general good health and strong well-disciplined body.

You have a tendency toward introspection and depression, and your health suffers as a consequence. You worry unnecessarily about small things, which is a drain on your energy. You must rid yourself of fear and uncertainty. You can counteract this by getting plenty of sunshine and leading an outdoor life. The company you keep will also influence your health, for you are happiest with youthful, energetic people.

A Capricorn woman's beauty is more than skin deep. Her physical attraction lasts long and becomes greater as life continues.

YOUR WORK: Your aim in life is to make a success of things. Reputation carries much weight with you, and you want to do work with some prestige and dignity attached

to it. Ambition is your driving force and often it is money—
or the promise of financial security—you are after when
you consider a position.

You believe that the road to progress lies through routine and adherence to precedent, but it is important that
you do not become a slave to routine and law and order.
After all, new methods are important to progress and you
should move with the times. You are not afraid of hard
work and are content to start at the bottom and work up.
Your rise to success is slow and difficult, but you are satisfied and do not expect it to be otherwise. As long as you
can see something at the end, you never falter. You stick
to it and get there in the end although it may be late in life.
Anything that is difficult and laborious interests you and
nothing is too hard or boring for you to tackle—and usually
with great success.

Being a natural diplomat, you are suited to politics. In
research, you are reliable and capable, but not brilliant.
In a managerial position, you can be happy systematizing
everything you come in contact with. Commerce attracts
you and you make a good craftsman, builder or practical
scientist.

Because you are bent on success and will take every opportunity that comes your way, you will not let anything or
anyone stop you and you may be unpopular with your fellow workers. However, duty means a lot to you and you
will always give good service. You take a great deal of
pride in what you do.

MONEY: Ambition being your strongest point, you apply
yourself to achieving monetary gains. The consolidation of
your affairs and resources is first and foremost in your mind
and to this end you are an opportunist on each and every
occasion.

Of all the signs of the Zodiac, yours imparts the greatest
desire for security. Sometimes you come up against frustrations in achieving this, which will make you give up
hope. After all, Capricorn is ruled by Saturn, and you are
pessimistic and somewhat gloomy by nature. You are
uncertain about yourself and your goals in life, but once
you have an objective, you go straight ahead.

You do not often speculate in money matters but are
slow and cautious, and you do not take chances. You are
industrious in making money and amass it slowly and
surely. You never waste anything and are always accurate
where money is concerned. You are trustworthy and will
take great pains with the affairs of someone whose finances
you are responsible for. The average Capricornian, when
young, is apt to be overcareful where money is concerned.
You always have the future in mind and put away for that
"rainy" day.

Later on, when you are more secure financially, your

attitude changes and you are very generous to all the people who have helped you. You find it a pleasure to help someone who has been in a position similar to your own.

YOUR HOME: Although you yearn for the security of a home, domesticity does not hold the appeal for you that it does for others. Your marriage is often the result of social reasons or professional ambition. Home life may take second place to your occupation and it is unlikely that you will want many children. You simply don't have enough time for them.

You feel the responsibility of parenthood very heavily. Your family ties are strong and underneath that distant manner which you may adopt towards those dear to you, there is great affection. You like to feel that you are needed and, once you have your own home, you expand in many ways. A marriage partner and children give you that special something you have been lacking and enable you to find what you have been searching for. You may not have even realized how much you need the warmth of family relationships. You are not nearly so much of a "lone wolf" as you sometimes think you are.

Your home exhibits evidence of your love of culture and the arts. You have a great love of music and anything that is beautiful and refined. Your surroundings reflect your personality. You feel that a peaceful atmosphere is essential for the smooth working of an efficient household. You should be careful about being too organized about everything and realize that you must relax once in a while. Don't be too much of a perfectionist.

You like privacy and are happy with the freedom it allows. You want your home to reflect your social status in the community and will work hard to beautify it. You like a lot of admiration and the feeling of prestige and inner satisfaction that it brings.

FRIENDSHIP: You are a person who has a wide circle of acquaintances but few close associations. You do not make friends easily, but are very good company when you forget your reserve and attempt to enjoy life. However, you do not mix easily and you envy those who find it natural. Any feeling of social awkwardness you may experience is the result of keeping people at a distance. This is really not a fault but simply your nature to keep people at arm's length. You are afraid of being hurt. You will climb alone on the long road to success.

You value your true friends highly. You will keep them for life and respect their secrets. You revel in sparkling company, which revives and inspires you. While you enjoy a certain amount of solitude, as mentioned above, you respond to companionship, which is necessary if you are to make real progress.

You like to keep abreast of affairs and are a good conversationalist. You are the type to join clubs and groups where you meet people, for you know the unhappiness that loneliness can bring. But it always takes a while for you to warm up to others enough to forget your inhibitions and let yourself become one of the crowd. Try to be less concerned with your own feelings.

People are not sure what you are thinking and you will never change in that respect. There is a corner of your heart that no one will ever see. As a child, others called you a "stick-in-the-mud" for you could never join in silly games and be one of the mob. As you get older, your loneliness and serious outlook will mellow and you will become wiser and more tolerant.

Those who really get to know you appreciate your friendship. You think it wise to steer clear of an argument for you like to keep the peace, but if you are pushed too far, you do "blow up." A violent quarrel may end a long relationship, and you will start off again on your ambitious way. You leave a job and end a friendship with the same forcefulness and are inspired anew with fresh plans. You never stand still.

ROMANCE: Although you are not especially romantic, this does not mean that you have no affections or feelings. You are intellectual rather than emotional in your approach to love-making. You are careful always to do the right thing and are very conscious of your partner's feelings. Your heart is governed by your mind and you have no time for flirtations.

You restrain yourself where love is concerned, and there is never any danger of someone being misled as to how you feel. You do not give away your affection until you are absolutely sure in your own mind that it is worthwhile. Although you are pretty sure about what you want, you do not often take the lead in romance. The affairs you do have are always sincere. You mean what you say.

You are inclined to put your career before romance and seldom let yourself go with anyone unless you can in some way benefit. It is difficult for those attracted to your charm to understand your hesitancy. You are secretive and do not reveal your real feelings. Once you make a decision, you are likely to end an attachment quickly, whereas you develop one slowly. You find love difficult to define and put it to one side, but you will still look for someone whom you can love and who will love you in return. You are ever hopeful where love is concerned.

You take life seriously and are a possessive lover easily made jealous. If anyone interferes with your love, you are more likely to feel robbed than emotionally hurt. You become cold and aloof and can "climb into your shell" when misunderstood or offended. It is difficult for you to show the deep affection which you may feel—no _matter how much you may want to show it.

Although what you are looking for may take some time to find, there is happiness in store for you as you are faithful in love. You are capable of making great sacrifices and are unchanging in your affections. Constancy is one of your strongest qualities.

MARRIAGE: You do not fall in love unless you are sure it is "the real thing," so it is likely that marriage will come late in life for you. You will have to search for the right one, and you are very selective in choosing your partner. Those who do not care for get the impression that you are being "choosy" and that you think you are "too good" for them. They call you a snob and are annoyed at your determination to find the right path. They think you are heartless when your selectiveness makes you discard people. They may feel that you are too idealistic and you may become depressed but your ambition carries you on, for it is one of the driving forces of your nature.

You attach great importance to the dignity of marriage and it plays a great part in your plans for the future. Despite your reserve, which will have to diminish if you are to find happiness, you need affection and companionship. An exciting partner who will keep you guessing is best suited to you. You should not expect all the attention you want from a quieter and more placid mate. Sometimes there is a difference in age and social standing between you and your partner.

It is important that your partner in marriage is with you all the way, for if you are dragged down in any manner, you will feel depressed and become moody. You will feel lonely, misunderstood and full of self-pity. It will be difficult for you both to make a go of things.

You may run the risk of neglecting your home and partner for outside interests. You like to play an active part in life around you and are inclined to think that there are other important things besides marriage. To be tied down to the routine of domestic life does not appeal to you. You are likely to become uncomfortable, for you like to lead a life of your own. If you find someone who permits you to do this, you will be satisfied and you will allow them to do likewise in return. In this way, you will both lead harmonious lives.

THE CAPRICORN HUSBAND is seldom a good emotional companion for his wife; he does not have the knack or willingness to give even a part of himself to create an atmosphere of enjoyment. He falls in readily with the domestic scheme, but adds little to its spiritual success. His basic nature is selfish; although there may be plenty of money, he will not allow his wife much domestic freedom of action. The entire household is directed by him, and he is often obstinate and unreasonable. His strict discipline may mean a smooth routine, but not necessarily a happy home.

He is usually a good provider, for he is very ambitious and successful in business most of the time. His selfish personality is tempered by those around him and it would be unfair to say that he is incapable of softer moods. He is often an agreeable person who enjoys a successful marriage in what others might consider a somewhat routine and pedestrian manner.

THE CAPRICORN WIFE is an efficient housekeeper who is a slave to duty. But men prefer less perfection and more warmth. She is an excellent cook and economist, a good hostess and is ambitious for her husband's and children's success in the world. She is an admirable woman although she is somewhat masculine in appearance and temperament.

She is ideal for the man who wishes his home life to run smoothly and who does not seek emotional or spiritual companionship. She is capable, faithful, dependable and systematic. She needs, most of all, encouragement and affection to call forth all of her deep loyalty which, once given, lasts a lifetime.

CHILDREN: You are basically fond of children although you will probably not have many. Outwardly, you may not be very affectionate, but your love for your children is very strong. You cherish those you have and are interested in them as individuals. You never underestimate their feelings or intelligence. Their welfare comes first, and you will work hard to give them a good education and fine start in life.

You have a strong sense of what is right and wrong, and woe betide your children when they overstep the mark. You are well-meaning in your discipline but should be careful of being too severe, which will only antagonize them. Nagging will break their spirits and there is only so much you can do to mold them into individuals capable of facing life. You sometimes forget that their childish ways need a little understanding and sympathy. They will be delighted when you unbend a little and play. So relax and join in the fun.

A Capricorn child is old for his age and apt to be too serious. They may be somewhat fearful and self-conscious and have few friends of their own age. They need a great deal of sympathy and affection. They need a lot of understanding and tact.

By now you are well aware that there are good and bad aspects to everyone's character, and that we can react to them or rectify them to our benefit.

If you are a good type of Capricornian, you may have the following characteristics:

POSITIVE QUALITIES: Your patience, perserverance and solidity are outstanding and you are always reliable. Serious-minded in your approach, you quietly go about whatever you have to do. You are modest in your tastes and the simple things in life give you much pleasure. You are fond of all that is old, for which you have great respect. Tradition and custom have a great influence on your life. You have both feet on the ground at all times and can exert great self-control if need be. You can apply yourself to almost any job with great industry and you seem to thrive on hard work.

You are very thoughtful of others and can prove a tower of strength to those weaker than yourself. You enjoy helping them and you can meet any demand made upon your resources. This adds to your confidence and optimism about the future. You also like a free hand to organize and use your keen business sense.

Your ambition must be given every opportunity, for if it is blocked, you will become miserable. It is your nature to organize your surroundings and those you come in contact with; in doing so you can bring about much good, not only for yourself but for others as well.

On the other hand, the lesser type of Capricornian may have these characteristics:

NEGATIVE QUALITIES: Like others, you have your faults. Your approach to life is too conventional and austere. Your urge to progress is held back by your old-fashioned ideas. You worry too much about the future instead of going forward to meet it. You have the ability and energy to cope with it, so do not be so pessimistic. You waste time being moody and tend to be indecisive.

Your desire for a high standing before the world and an important place in society sometimes makes you too materialistic. You take advantage of others, and the resulting benefits make you greedy and lead to downright selfishness and craftiness. You are sometimes carried away by thriftiness to the extent of meanness.

You are severe with yourself and others, and your friends sometimes find you cold and standoffish. You lessen your chance of meeting interesting people by being too critical and cautious. You have to learn to see another's viewpoint.

You are often hard to please and are easily disappointed when you do not get what you want. You are afraid of being overshadowed and want recognition of your superiority. You should control your calculating nature and moderate your urge to manage others.

If you can get over your fear of ridicule, you will stop nursing grievances for so long. You find it hard to forgive anyone who has harmed you, even when the injury is unintentional.

To "know yourself" is the secret of a happy, well-adjusted mind and way of life. You have the ability to understand your faults; it is up to you to overcome them.

Capricorn compatible with Aquarius, Pisces, Taurus, Virgo, Scorpio, Sagittarius.

Incompatible with Aries, Cancer, Libra.

Aquarius

CHARACTER ANALYSIS FOR PEOPLE BORN BETWEEN JANUARY 20—FEBRUARY 18

OF ALL people you are the most unselfish. You love humanity and value peace very highly. In your make-up is the desire to change any condition in life that appears to you unhealthy or lacking in progress. You always aim for the highest in human harmony, and anything less causes you unhappiness. In matters of human conduct it may be said that, of all types, you are the most nearly above reproach.

You like to have a useful hobby. You may take a great interest in advanced theories of education. You want to bring luxury and privilege to every person, and you also want everyone to have the intellectual background to understand and appreciate great and good things. You have a deep sympathy for poverty, but you have a deeper concern for ignorance. You want to raise the mental standard of the whole world. It is more important to you that everyone thinks rather than eats. Perhaps you instinctively know that man will eat, but must be trained to love or think. You feel that when men are responsible mentally, there will be happiness for everybody.

You are always miles ahead of others in new thoughts and original approaches to problems, and you are always willing to accept new designs for living. You have a strong urge to develop along creative lines, whether the results are the establishment of new businesses, new ideas or an inspiring love affair.

Group interests and humanity at large are what concern you most in life. The problems of an individual never interest you too deeply. But, nevertheless, people like to confide in you and ask your advice.

People never know for certain what you are going to do next. You have an unusual detachment, as if you were observing everything and everybody. For this reason you are very tolerant and do not demand that others do what you want. You seem to be everything at the same time: conventional and eccentric, fond of tradition and fond of all that is new.

Sometimes you feel that ordinary laws are not for you, and you may go through a period of wanting to be unusual and of doing everything that is irregular. You may not want to dress like other people and may develop special mannerisms and styles of your own. You always like to be completely individual in what you say and do.

YOUR HEALTH: You are strong and can resist sickness in spite of your delicate build. You look, and generally are, exceedingly fit and healthy. This is due to the fact that you are sensible about cleanliness and have healthy habits, so that disease rarely gets a chance to attack you.

You should not allow yourself to be intimidated by others, nor should you let the strain of opposition take too much out of you in health and strength. Diet and vitamins will counteract your intense nervousness; good food, fresh air and peaceful surroundings will keep you well. Since you are a naturally placid person, you know instinctively how to stand up to opposition without letting it affect your health or disposition.

The state of mind in which you approach your work will also affect your health. And pressure from worry is often what starts illness. It would be wise to exercise your natural ability to view all things objectively, so that you will achieve harmony and peace of mind. If you meet small disturbances philosophically, they will take less out of you. You can definitely train yourself to control your mind.

Physically your weak points are the calves and ankles, and you should take care that these parts of the body are not injured. You may suffer from nervous disturbances and circulation troubles, such as anemia, low blood pressure and similar ailments. It is most important that your blood be kept in good condition.

Aquarians are usually pleasant-looking people. They have graceful, medium-sized figures, well-shaped heads, broad foreheads indicating intelligence, and a sympathetic expression. Everything about them is moderate, so that it is difficult to describe their physique. Usually their eyes are their most outstanding feature.

An Aquarian woman has an unusual fascination all of her own. She is imaginative and intellectual and frequently steals the show from others more beautiful than she.

YOUR WORK: You like to be busy in some useful work, which must always have a touch of culture and idealism about it. You never choose an uninteresting job as a life work; whatever it is, you invest it with new life and give it an individual slant that often pays financially.

Work agrees with you. You can accomplish a great deal in a little time and with half the energy that most people put into a job. You are naturally an able person and frequently suggest some improvement in method in whatever you take on. You can handle responsibility but dislike taking orders.

Your brain is always working on some invention or completely original idea, and anything that is different intrigues you. Routine work wears you down, for you prefer something unusual. You like to leave routine jobs to others and generally work in fits and starts. You are quick on the uptake but are often careless.

Slow and stupid people make you impatient. You may be intolerant towards them if they have fewer natural talents than you, though you are always ready to make life easier for others. But your sympathy for people who have less than you, whether materially or mentally, keeps you from being openly critical.

You are the most suitable of all types to carry out social service work, for you care more for people in general than for yourself. Aquarians are valuable people to have in rehabilitation work. They are found in every successful ministering group, from the highest to the lowest position.

If you are the intellectual type of Aquarian, you make a fine writer, for you have a keen sense of the dramatic. Anything out of the ordinary fascinates you, so that you have the ability of weaving interesting plots.

You may have a special fondness for the arts and may become a connoisseur of painting, music and literature. Most of you are gifted in some way and may have a particular aptitude or talent for some art.

You should put every ounce of effort into your creative work, to achieve that high standard you aim at. You will do well in any work where you can use your imagination. You do not do so well in your own business, as you are too much of a dreamer. You may not act quickly enough and let things slide.

MONEY: Money is a means to an end. You can be both lucky and unlucky. You are neither extravagant or indulgent; you like money for what it can buy in the way of progress and development for the work you are doing.

You are most likely to make money through your inventions and discoveries. It will require long, patient effort, but the thought and work of today will bring you wealth tomorrow. You have ambition and talent but do not always make the most of them.

You would rather have success come to you instead of making practical plans to go out for it. Wealth and honors are quite acceptable to you, but you may not feel that their achievement is worth the necessary labor.

YOUR HOME: Your home and family must never possess you and, while you have a deep feeling for them, you still manage to maintain your independence. You are not the type to center your interests and attention on your home or possessions.

You like a nice home where you can entertain, for you are very sociable. It is likely to be modern in style and artistically furnished. It will have the most modern appliances; every labor-saving device possible, because you see no reason to waste time or energy in housework. You will enjoy bringing home the latest useful invention and demonstrating it to your admiring family. No old-fashioned methods for you—you must have every timesaving device that your money allows.

Too much activity in your home annoys you, for you like to be by yourself now and then. You like social life and join clubs and societies, but you also like solitude. You have a strong need for it and like to withdraw into yourself. It is then that you are able to appreciate the arts, which play such an important part in your life.

FRIENDSHIPS: You are a cheerful soul and quite at home in company. Of all types you make the best friends. In your relations with friends, business associates and loved ones you are at your best. You enjoy human contacts and are very friendly. But often you are an unusual type whom few understand really well. You may even seem cold and aloof to some, because you stand apart. Although you may form many associations, your temperament is often too detached to make many warm and intimate friendships. There are many recluses born under this sign and you may allow yourself to become unapproachable.

You see good in everything, manage to get along with everyone and seldom find fault with any person, no matter how badly they treat you. But you will not martyr yourself unnecessarily and, if imposed upon in any way, you will make sure that the other person realizes that you do not like it.

Your willingness to accept as friends eccentric and colorful characters sometimes has bad results, for you are easily influenced and inclined to trust everyone, and always believe a hard-luck story. You may be deceived and suffer loss as a consequence. This is never a lesson for you, for you like to study your fellow man at close quarters. You are always eager to observe human conduct under all kinds of conditions. A person is never entirely bad to you, even when he is openly corrupt.

You are always willing to give a great deal of yourself and usually receive considerable satisfaction in return. Your friendship is appreciated by all those who have the privilege of knowing you. Friendship with you has an inspiring quality that helps to raise every relationship to its highest form.

You are loyal to your acquaintances and, when you are understood, keep true friendships throughout life. They are dear and close to you, and you realize that these associations form one of the bases of life. Your friends appreciate the way you do not meddle in their affairs, for you know that too much intimacy breeds contempt. Aquarius is the sign of the brotherhood of man.

ROMANCE: You have a slight tendency to prefer universal love to personal love and romance may be as much a meeting of mentalities as hearts. Usually you look for some mutual mental interest in your loved one and, when you do find an intellectual companion who appeals to you, you are faithful forever.

You may seek an ideal person, one whose intellectual and emotional resources equal your own. You will not tolerate anything else and, if your loved one does not measure up to your standards, you may fall out of love without any explanation.

You are attractive to the opposite sex and may have many romances because you are often in love with love and may not know your own mind. Your heart may rule your head and, as you do things on impulse, you may make mistakes.

You are not usually excessively affectionate. In comparison with warm and passionate lovers, you may seem quite cold. However, you have your own rules, and your strong sense of personal liberty makes you a difficult person to possess. You usually demand a large measure of freedom and seclusion in romance and marriage. You never give up your privacy or your right to do as you please. Underneath this urge for expression of your free will, you are strongly affectionate. Although you do not show it readily, you are sensitive and can be led but never driven. A partner who understands your true nature will enjoy your love to the full.

MARRIAGE: Although you do not have a strong inclination towards marriage, you make one of the best partners, either in business or marriage, of any of the signs. You seldom do anything to cause discord, and your good sense and practical outlook do much to avert it. You need intellectual and spiritual companionship if your marriage is to be a success.

Your married life will usually be peaceful, and you are strongly attached to your mate over a long period. You do not want to be boss and run the household, but you resent enforced obedience. Apart from this, you are usually faithful and constant. You love your family but sometimes, when you are busy with other matters, they may feel that you are losing interest in them.

Both sexes may enter into a marriage of convenience quite happily if they feel that there is a mental attraction. They may both live happily if their partners accept their belief that there are other interests in the world besides love.

If your partner does not object to your aloofness and the way in which you withdraw, it will be an excellent partnership. If your partner's intellect is on the same level as your own, you will not grow bored.

THE AQUARIAN HUSBAND is one of the most kind and generous of all types. He will not try to run the household or attempt to interfere with existing conditions. His is an openhanded spirit, and giving without thought of return or reward is part of his character. He is always considerate, a perfect gentleman in every way. He treats his wife and family with the same consideration that he shows to strangers. He is not normally an ardent lover, but accepts marriage as part of the domestic scheme. As he is gracious, cooperative and understands the need for harmony, marriage is usually a success with him.

Sometimes his impersonal attitude is a drawback in marriage. Many women seem to prefer the somewhat selfish dominance of the more aggressive type to his broad-minded attitude. It seems more a lack of interest, particularly to self-centered wives who want all the attention of their husbands. The Aquarian man's domestic life would be far more successful if he were married to a highly intellectual woman whose work in the world is as important as his own broad interests.

THE AQUARIAN WIFE may not slip into matrimony with ease but she is better equipped for it than others. She is capable, intellectual, discerning, adaptable and often very talented. She has a man's ability to accomplish a day's work without grumbling and fatigue, coupled with the ability to be a fine housekeeper.

She attracts people with her easy manner, makes her home a social center and has wide interests. It would never occur to her to watch her husband's actions with suspicion or try to check up on how he spends his spare time. She naturally trusts him. Her own behavior is beyond reproach. She is one of the kindest people in the world and would rather suffer herself than cause others unhappiness.

She is basically an unconventional woman. Should she wish to change partners, and be sufficiently justified in doing so, she will make the change without hesitation.

Emotionally she is very responsive, but her intellect rules her, and she is most appreciated as a wife when married to an intelligent man whose work she can share and who is able to use her abilities on his own behalf.

CHILDREN: You do not look down on children but treat them as individuals, and they respect you in return. You treat them in an intelligent way and so give them the confidence which brings out their natural abilities.

You have an affinity to children, as there is something strangely immature about you. They quickly find out that you have a wonderful supply of stories and games. You are well able to cope with their childish ways and will not stand for any nonsense. They are usually well-behaved in your company, for they find they cannot upset you easily.

Aquarian children should never be treated as anything other than equals. They are the most interesting youngsters, but in many ways the most difficult. They have to be treated as chums and companions and have to be given wise reasons why they should or should not do certain things. Their natural aptitudes should be encouraged and they should be urged to project their original ideas and thoughts.

By now you are well aware that there are good and bad aspects to everyone's character, and that we can react to them or rectify them to our benefit. If you are a good type of Aquarian, you may have the following characteristics:

POSITIVE QUALITIES: You are a quiet, humane individual with a basic ideal of the "brotherhood of man," which accounts for your Bohemian tastes.

You have a straightforward nature and, although your temper is not to be overlooked, you seldom bear any malice. You can be genial and amusing; you are strong-willed and pursue an object with great determination.

Your achievements will be due to your devotion to duty. You like to travel a good deal for all sorts of reasons. You like movement of all kinds, and your own personality easily adapts itself to ardent causes.

Truth and sincerity are your strong points. You have a brilliant mind, with inventive ability, and can make much of your life if you resist the temptation to become a dreamer and do not allow yourself to drift. You know what you should be doing, but it is easier sometimes to find excuses for not doing it.

On the other hand, the lesser type of Aquarian may have the following characteristics:

NEGATIVE QUALITIES: Although you have many of the likeable qualities of the strong Aquarian, you lack his constructive ability. You lack common sense and spend much time in abstract thought.

You can be destructive, for you stir up conditions of discontent and dissatisfaction in your environment. With many assurances that all is well, you proceed merrily along, lacking the ability to adjust matters. You can talk yourself into good jobs and then proceed to hold them by fooling the boss. You may be erratic and unreliable, and your incapability is usually revealed by some accident. You may make so much trouble by your nosiness, tiresome interference and upsetting point of view that it takes the combined efforts of a good many people to undo the confusion created.

Your natural aloofness often makes you oblivious to the reactions of others. Your independence may be resented and you may easily become touchy and argumentative. Your offensiveness makes you unpopular and breaks up your friendships.

Pride and vanity are your weaknesses and you hate to be criticized. You plan to make your way through life under your own steam, guided by your own convictions, so that often your way is contrary to that of everyone else. You are too sensitive about personal remarks and you can take umbrage over the smallest details and become suspicious.

Although you have progressive ideas, they may be ultra-modern. You may not be particularly enterprising and, if you do strike out, it is often in some uncommon pursuit which may be unconventional in the bad sense. Many consider your disposition to be peculiar and incalculable. You would be more successful if you were a little more practical and less idealistic.

Aquarius compatible with Pisces, Aries, Gemini, Libra, Sagittarius, Capricorn.

Incompatible with Taurus, Leo, Scorpio.

Pisces

CHARACTER ANALYSIS FOR PEOPLE BORN BETWEEN FEBRUARY 19—MARCH 20

YOU HAVE an unusual dual personality which sometimes puzzles others as well as yourself. You are dreamy, responsive, impressionable, and have a sensitive approach to life. You are gentle, but are completely unrealistic and often lack the ability to cope with the conditions of everyday life. You are timid and have no self-confidence and find it difficult to make up your own mind. People find you honest, conscientious and trustworthy. You are very likable and have a sweet temper, but you run the risk of letting others take advantage of you, for you are peaceable by nature and prefer not to fight back. You generally have many friends, but often they hurt your feelings and you are quick to take offense where none was intended. You should try to be more understanding.

You are methodical in what you do and you make sure that you do no work unless it is absolutely necessary. You are able to accept what life brings and you like changes, especially if they help the betterment of mankind, for you are altruistic by nature.

Your sympathy knows no bounds and you know exactly how the other person feels. You see clearly what is wrong with the world and, in your vivid imagination, you have all sorts of plans to improve it. It is a pity that you seldom have the power to put your plans into action. When you do accomplish them, a great service is rendered to the world, but more often than not you are a dreamer who is frustrated in your efforts.

Sometimes your spiritual retreats from the world result in beautiful creative work in music, poetry or painting. You love the unknown and mysterious, but often it clashes with the basic urges in your character and you find it difficult to adjust yourself to life. You are very susceptible to the ideas of others and any theory is likely to get a hold on you. Your understanding of these theories and your extraordinary perception may give you a feeling of isolation, even superiority.

Your moods vary from the highest to the lowest and you are inclined to more self-pity than is good for you. This could cause you to avoid any issue that crops up, for you are able to give confidence to others, but when it comes to facing facts yourself, you often bring about disorder. When faced with the truth, you will never admit it and will find some sort of excuse. You may shirk responsibility and, as a rule, cannot stand alone, yet encouragement from others may completely restore your self-confidence and an optimistic outlook.

YOUR HEALTH: Physically you are not robust and your constitution is not as strong as other signs, so that you do not resist disease. Yet when you are ill, you will take care of yourself and you readily respond to treatment. You need a firm physician in whom you have confidence because you are so impressionable. But you often have natural good health and are best suited to an out-of-doors life. The more exercise you get the better, as long as it is not too strenuous. Frequently you look younger than you are and live to quite a fair age.

Your feet and respiratory system are the parts of your body most easily affected by ill health. Being somewhat subject to colds, you should guard against going about with wet feet or sitting in drafts or neglecting any symptoms of lung trouble.

Moderation in every way should be your guiding principle, and to stick to this rule, you will have to take a firm grip on yourself. Most of your illnesses are the result of overindulgence, so watch your diet carefully. You are attracted to any form of physical stimulation and, for this reason, should not make liquor or sedatives a habit. As you are quite often headstrong, you may not realize the dangers of this.

Should you become a victim of habit, you may not have the will power to fight back. You like to be pitied and love to regard yourself as the victim of circumstances. Naturally, this makes life difficult for yourself and others. You have an excellent chance of leading an even longer life and will look younger and feel younger than your years if you take sufficiently good care of yourself.

Pisceans usually have a slim and frail physique and make very good dancers. Often they have an ethereal look about them, almost elfin, with large, dreamy eyes and fine hair. Their bones are small and they have exceptionally lovely feet and hands.

YOUR WORK: Your main aim in life is to help other people. You are naturally attracted to the needy and the sick and are best suited to teaching, nursing, catering, book-keeping, accounting, entertaining or welfare work. You have a wealth of sympathy and understanding to offer; anything or anyone needing help draws you to them. You may be a social worker.

The work you finally select should provide you with the opportunity to exercise your strong power of insight into others' problems. You are also suited to diplomatic work and any job requiring discretion and charm.

You have a "plastic" nature that can be molded into many shapes. You have leanings in many directions and, as there are two sides to your character, there are other types of work suitable for you. The stage, screen and radio are also fields that you might explore. Here your artistry and active imagination will come into play. You may be thoroughly at home with music, writing, poetry and plays, and any of the arts. You are successful because you have the ability to absorb and clearly express the emotions of others.

Your talents are varied and, therefore, you will probably be happy with variety in your work. If you have the right job, your sensitive nature is fortified against the frustrations which you will meet.

You are not happy doing detailed work where much concentration is required. Yet you possess a good deal of determination when doing something your whole heart is in. Whenever hard work is required, you are loyal, industrious and methodical. You have the knack of taking short cuts and surprise others by your timesaving methods of reaching your goal. You are good company and generally get on well with your fellow workers.

On the other hand, you may become lazy. Any discouragement you get can throw you into complete confusion and you will be thoroughly disorganized. There are times when you just cannot seem to think straight. You act as if you are "going around in circles."

MONEY: Your sensitive feelings respond to the pleasures and comforts of the material things in life. Usually you do not want money just for the sake of having it, but fundamentally you set great stock on the security it brings. You are conscious of approaching old age and the danger of being dependent.

Lack of funds is a great worry to you and hampers your progress. Through helping others you often become involved in their problems and you may find yourself giving away or spending more than you should. You will probably never have a great deal of money, and if you do, it will probably be wheedled away from you by conniving relatives or those who need help. It is difficult for you to refuse any request or plea and you are, therefore, an easy target for craving sympathy.

As you sometimes do not know what you want or why you want it, it is often difficult for you to set yourself a goal and work towards it. However, once you have decided on a goal, you can find the determination to pursue it. Some of you may have good luck where finance is concerned. You would be wise to put money safely in real estate or something tangible, rather than investing where there is a gamble. Lack of funds is a great worry to you and hampers your progress.

You have good business sense, but are not equipped by nature to enter the competitive business world. You can be of great help to a business, but need as a partner someone who can battle for you. When it comes to entertaining and caring for others, nothing is too much trouble and you spare no expense.

YOUR HOME: Environment is vital to success, and success in your case is mostly a matter of personal adjustments to your surroundings. Like most people, you need a place where you can relax and let your imagination have full play. If you are to improve your lot in life, a home and family are essential. Your dual nature may even lead to two homes or two sets of families.

You are essentially a home-loving person and like neatness and order and the simple things in life. You enjoy an unsophisticated existence and do not continually seek entertainment outside. You like a country life and plenty of freedom so that you can roam at will. Your surroundings will reflect your love of the arts and you will be happiest when you have a free hand to show your appreciation of them.

Generally, your home is a place where friends are always welcome. They know they will always find good conversation and a sympathetic listener to their troubles. It is also a place of peace and comfort, for you dislike disturbances of any kind.

You like to keep an active interest in outside affairs, such as charitable work. There is every chance of your enjoying a happy family life if you do, as long as it does not interfere with your routine in the home.

FRIENDSHIPS: Your warmth of heart and personal magnetism attract many friends. They find you gentle, helpful and kind, and are sometimes inclined to take advantage of your good nature. They sap your energy and resources, but still you are always ready for self-sacrifice. "To have a friend you must be a friend" is your firm belief, and you take every opportunity to put this into practice. People will want to confide in you and "cry on your shoulder" because you are a good listener and understand their problems. You appreciate their troubles because of your deep perception of human feelings and failings. You worry when they worry and laugh when they laugh. You have deep sense of empathy.

You are loyal to your friends and respect and value their acquaintance. Sometimes you may be "snowed under" with obligations that you will always fulfill, and they will take their toll of you physically. Your friendships may become too close and often "familiarity breeds contempt." You may be altogether too peaceful, valuing harmony above all, and yield to others' wishes. Your individuality becomes swamped, and in the back of your mind you sense this and become dissatisfied. People will still respect you if you assert yourself a little more. True friends will not hurt you, for they realize that you are very sensitive to harmful criticism.

ROMANCE: Of all natures, yours is the most sensitive and romance and marriage mean much to you. You are sincere and affectionate, and dislike meanness or pettiness. Your standards are high and you look for someone who is careful of her appearance, intelligent and has some artistic ability. You can be jealous of your loved one and suspicion will kill your love. You should enjoy your love more and not look for too much perfection.

You are the type who needs much assurance of your loved one's affection, with plenty of flattery and compliments. Your feelings are hurt much too easily, and you may let your sensitivity needlessly break up a romance. Also, your will power and ability to make up your mind are often weak, so that frequently you do not know what you want in romance.

Sometimes you are a dreamer possessing high ideals and aspirations and, with the right person behind you, there is more chance of their materializing. Without love, life is empty for you. Often you waste more time dreaming about love than really doing something constructive to gain it. You seldom possess a strong individual character, and live largely on the thoughts and feelings of those you come in contact with. That is why it is important for you to choose the right mate.

You are capable of deep feeling and emotion, and once your affection is given, it is everlasting. Often you have difficulty in saying "No," so you should be careful of being led into an affair against your will with a stronger personality than your own. Your moods may cause your loved one to be unsure of how you really feel, for you can be cold and aloof one moment and warm and affectionate the next. Although you take romance and love seriously, often it is hard for another to realize you are in earnest in your love affairs.

When you know your own weakness, you try to adopt a second and harder skin. You will put on a rough and sharp front, whereas inside you are gentle, kind and touchy. A person who is really sincere and has a true understanding of you will see this and will not be put off by your secretiveness. They know you are only trying to cover up what you do not want others to see.

MARRIAGE: In love and marriage the Piscean is at home. It is a warm and delightful association for you. Your natural urge is to serve mankind and there is no other type of person that makes a better wife or mother. Both male and female love domestic life and thrive in the atmosphere of a happy home. The romantic side of marriage appeals more to you than to most people, and this will continue right through life.

Within the home you are dependable, show great affection and flatter your mate with little attentions and gestures of affection. You are courteous and considerate of the comfort and pleasure of your partner. You are generally easy to get along with. You are more apt to dissolve into tears than become silent and moody when disagreements arise.

THE PISCES HUSBAND is most loving, attentive, considerate, thoughtful, and never forgets to treat his wife with courtesy. His romantic and imaginative outlook is affected by the proximity of others and, being impressionable, he is liable to be attracted to outside temptations. The more positive type of Piscean is able to keep his mind occupied with other interests. He is contemplative and fond of study. He has the ability and the intellect to combine two ways of earning a living and lead a happy married life as well.

Pisces is the sign of the artist and author, so that you can also earn your bread and butter by an additional occupation which suits your tastes and capabilities, and still lead a happy married life.

The Pisces husband is not a good provider. Although he is generous in giving what he has, there are times when his desire for future security may cause him to be "tight" with the money his wife wants to spend. He seems to have no idea of reality and feels the difficulties of life to be almost unconquerable. He lives in a phantom world, which makes difficult the household's struggle for existence. If he has good advice and the direction to know what work suits him best and the initiative to find it, he will make a good husband.

THE PISCES WIFE has deep spiritual qualities and emotional responses which make her ideally adapted to domestic life. She can provide the spiritual and emotional escape which is valued so highly by most men. She will make the kindest, most loving, devoted and sympathetic of wives. She can easily adjust herself, is extremely responsive and makes an excellent mate. She is a restful wife for a husband to come home to. She is the kind of wife a husband always wants to come home to.

Often the Pisces wife is not as active as others, or as capable, and she has a tendency to let housework slide. She has a great sense of comfort and studies the home so that it will be as restful as possible. But she is often not very practical in her good intentions and they may be a bit fanciful. If she is the self-indulgent type, she may waste a lot of time seeking pleasure and entertainment or just taking it easy. She may play cards or join women's clubs or go to movies a lot.

If her health is delicate, she will need the greatest determination to keep herself optimistic and mentally alert. But the Pisces wife is a fine antidote for the tired business-man and wage earner.

CHILDREN: You like to have children around you and place great importance on giving them a good education and start in life. You adore children and they will adore you. If anything, you spoil them and give in too easily. If you adopt a firm attitude towards them, it will pay dividends. If you do not take too much notice of their playful ways, there is less risk of their taking advantage of your sensitivity, so be definite in what you want right from the start. Your imagination makes you a great storyteller. You also like to make up and act in children's plays. You are an adult to whom fantasy is real, and children appreciate and respond to this side of your nature.

Piscean children live in a world of fantasy all their own. Make-believe is important to them and they are highly susceptible to its influence. It can be made an excellent means of education for them, and a teacher can use it successfully to make the most ordinary problems exciting and less difficult.

Generally, Piscean children are able to carry on an interesting conversation at an early age and are excellent company. They show an early aptitude for the arts and should become very versatile if their teachers and parents set about it in the right way.

By now you are well aware that there are good and bad aspects to everyone's character, and that we can react to them or rectify them to our benefit.

If you are a good type of Piscean, you may have the following characteristics:

POSITIVE QUALITIES: You have an active sympathy for mankind, which is the driving force behind everything you do. Your virtues are more passive than active and, given the right kind of friends and an encouraging environment, you can achieve great heights. You have a true and direct conception of life and the knack of taking short cuts to truth and wisdom.

You are sensitive, with an unusual power of intuition, and are intelligent enough to make good use of it. Your mind is always receptive to new ideas and methods, and anything that will make the world a better place to live in. You are an idealist and believe that everyone can be happy with a little cooperation. You are prepared to do your part and will help others in their search for a well-balanced and constructive life.

You have a serenity of mind which makes it possible for you to accept what life brings you, but you should take care not to become too moody and simply drift along with the tide.

On the other hand, a lesser type of Piscean may have these characteristics:

NEGATIVE QUALITIES: You are unnecessarily pessimistic and full of self-pity. You have a feeling of persecution, that people are always trying to get the better of you. You feel misunderstood and the world seems cruel. You withdraw into yourself and feel depressed. This is the result of worrying too much over petty slights that do not really amount to much. This is quite disastrous to your delicate nature. Aimlessness of thought and action is a favorite and all-too-frequent pastime of yours. Keep your sights on what is truly important in life.

If you realize that you are your own worst enemy and that you can quite easily get over this sense of isolation, you will be more happily adjusted. People are not as hostile and unsympathetic as you think. You like to be needed and to have people draw upon your wonderful resources of sympathy and understanding. It is up to you to make them available to others, not to cut yourself off from contact with humanity. You are likely to do this if your supersensitive nature is subjected to hurts inflicted by the wrong type of company.

Do not be overly timid, but learn to have faith in yourself. You will then be confident in discriminating among whom and what you like and dislike. You should realize all your many good points and how your faults can undermine them, and that with courage you can overcome the obstacles that come your way. Who knows the success that may come your way when you blossom out with strength of purpose behind you.

Pisces compatible with Aries, Taurus, Cancer, Scorpio, Capricorn, Aquarius.

Incompatible with Gemini, Virgo, Sagittarius.